I CAN READ TAROT

A BEGINNERS GUIDE TO LEARNING TAROT

With tips and suggestions for the visual learner

ELISA SOFO

First published in 2020

Copyright @ Elisa Sofo

All rights reserved. No part of this book may be reproduced or transmitted in any form or by any means, electronic or mechanical, including photocopying recording or by any information storage and retrieval system, without prior permission in writing from the publisher.

Illustrations from the Rider-Waite Tarot Deck® reproduced by permission of U.S. Games Systems, Inc., Stamford, CT 06902 USA. Copyright ©1971 by U.S. Games Systems, Inc. Further reproduction prohibited. The Rider-Waite Tarot Deck® is a registered trademark of U.S. Games Systems, Inc.

Images from Authors own 1970 A.E.Waite deck. Drawn by Pamela Coleman Smith and printed by Rider & Company, London.

Image reproduction and technical assistance by Brad Slater

ISBN 978-0-6487355-0-2

Published by Perfect Timing Tarot
www.perfecttimingtarot.com.au
Email: perfecttimingtarot@outlook.com

Cover design by Brad Slater
Formatting by Polgarus Studio

Dedicated to my family whose support improves my life and to Sally and Ray Carr whose support has helped shape my life.

Contents

Introduction 1
Getting Started 5

0 - Fool 6
The Magician - 1 8
The High Priestess - 2 10
The Empress - 3 12
The Emperor – 4 14
The Hierophant - 5 16
The Lovers - 6 18
The Chariot - 7 20
Strength - 8 22
The Hermit - 9 24
Wheel of Fortune - 10 26
Justice - 11 28
The Hanged Man - 12 30
Death - 13 32
Temperance - 14 34
The Devil - 15 36
The Tower - 16 38
The Star - 17 40
The Moon - 18 42
The Sun – 19 44
Judgement - 20 46
The World - 21 48
Ace of Wands 50
Two of Wands 52
Three of Wands 54
Four of Wands 56
Five of Wands 58
Six of wands 60
Seven of Wands 62
Eight of Wands 64
Nine of Wands 66
Ten of Wands 68
Page of Wands 70

Knight of wands	72
Queen of Wands	74
King of Wands	76
Ace of Pentacles	78
Two of Pentacles	80
Three of Pentacles	82
Four of Pentacles	84
Five of Pentacles	86
Six of Pentacles	88
Seven of Pentacles	90
Eight of Pentacles	92
Nine of Pentacles	94
Ten of Pentacles	96
Page of Pentacles	98
Knight of Pentacles	100
Queen of Pentacles	102
King of Pentacles	104
Ace of Cups	106
Two of Cups	108
Three of Cups	110
Four of Cups	112
Five of Cups	114
Six of Cups	116
Seven of Cups	118
Eight of Cups	120
Nine of Cups	122
Ten of Cups	124
Page of Cups	126
Knight of Cups	128
Queen of Cups	130
King of Cups	132
Ace of Swords	134
Two of Swords	136
Three of Swords	138
Four of Swords	140
Five of Swords	142
Six of Swords	144
Seven of Swords	146
Eight of Swords	148
Nine of Swords	150
Ten of Swords	152
Page of Swords	154
Knight of Swords	156
Queen of Swords	158
King of Swords	160

Getting to know your deck 163
Major Arcana 165
Minor Arcana 168
A little on Numerology 171
Colours of the Tarot 173
Symbols on The Cards 175
Exercises for the Visual Learner 177
Drawing Cards for a Reading 179
Spreads 181
Frequently Asked Questions - FAQ's 186

Reversals 195
The Fool Reversed 196
The Magician Reversed 197
The High Priestess Reversed 198
The Empress Reversed 199
The Emperor Reversed 200
The Hierophant Reversed 201
The Lovers Reversed 202
The Chariot Reversed 203
Strength Reversed 204
The Hermit Reversed 205
Wheel of Fortune Reversed 206
Justice Reversed 207
The Hanged Man Reversed 208
Death Reversed 209
Temperance Reversed 210
The Devil Reversed 211
The Tower Reversed 212
The Star Reversed 213
The Moon Reversed 214
The Sun Reversed 215
Judgement Reversed 216
The World Reversed 217
Ace of Wands Reversed 218
Two of Wands Reversed 219
Three of Wands Reversed 220
Four of Wands Reversed 221
Five of Wands Reversed 222
Six of Wands Reversed 223
Seven of Wands Reversed 224
Eight of Wands Reversed 225
Nine of Wands Reversed 226
Ten of Wands Reversed 227
Page of Wands Reversed 228
Knight of Wands Reversed 229

Queen of Wands Reversed 230
King of Wands Reversed 231
Ace of Pentacles Reversed 232
Two of Pentacles Reversed 233
Three of Pentacles Reversed 234
Four of Pentacles Reversed 235
Five of Pentacles Reversed 236
Six of Pentacles Reversed 237
Seven of Pentacles Reversed 238
Eight of Pentacles Reversed 239
Nine of Pentacles Reversed 240
Ten of Pentacles Reversed 241
Page of Pentacles Reversed 242
Knight of Pentacles Reversed 243
Queen of Pentacles Reversed 244
King of Pentacles Reversed 245
Ace of Cups Reversed 246
Two of Cups Reversed 247
Three of Cups Reversed 248
Four of Cups Reversed 249
Five of Cups Reversed 250
Six of Cups Revered 251
Seven of Cups Reversed 252
Eight of Cups Reversed 253
Nine of Cups Reversed 254
Ten of Cups Reversed 255
Page of Cups Reversed 256
Knight of Cups Reversed 257
Queen of Cups Reversed 258
King of Cups Reversed 259
Ace of Swords Reversed 260
Two of Swords Reversed 261
Three of Swords Reversed 262
Four of Swords Reversed 263
Five of Swords Reversed 264
Six of Swords Reversed 265
Seven of Swords Reversed 266
Eight of Swords Reversed 267
Nine of Swords Reversed 268
Ten of Swords Reversed 269
Page of Swords Reversed 270
Knight of Swords Reversed 271
Queen of Swords Reversed 272
King of Swords Reversed 273

Conclusion 275

Introduction

"Please help me!"
"I want to learn tarot, but I don't know where to start."
"Can you recommend a good book?"

Does this sound like you?

This is something I've heard over and over again and it has troubled me. Sure, there are many, many books out there available to the beginner, lots of them very good and informative, but through my research, and also through my own experiences early on, they can just be words on paper and the ability to retain all the information is often overwhelming and difficult, especially for the more visual learner.

This leads me to explaining the concept of this book. Throughout the tarot community the quest to find an easy and effective way to just **begin** is becoming an issue. Experienced Tarot readers wanting advice on how to teach their child or young adult, the more mature person who has always had an interest in tarot but have never known where to start, and everyone in between who has felt the pull or draw of the cards, are all out there searching for an easy and straightforward way to learn.

It is often said in tarot circles that key meanings are not the way to learn tarot, but instead we must look at the cards and let them talk to us through our intuition. I have to apologise to all those who I am now disagreeing with, but I firmly believe this to be a mistruth in part. I believe, and find, to be a more effective process for becoming a practiced reader, is to first comprehend the key meanings and work with those key meanings as the initial step in your tarot education. Intuition does play a major role in being a good card reader, rather than an average one who relies only on key meanings, but we do need to get to know our cards and what they represent as a whole before relying on our intuition to draw out the subtleties within the images on the cards.

When I started on my mission to learn, I went to a new age bookstore and headed to the Tarot card section. I picked up a copy of the Rider Waite Smith deck, as advised by the lovely lady who worked there. I also picked out a book believing it was the right book to teach me given its Rider Waite image on the cover. Wrong! It is a great reference book, years on now that I am a seasoned reader, but at the time, it was just a whole lot of information that I didn't understand.

I persevered, such was my desire to learn and, as is often the way, thanks to the Universe, I stumbled across an online beginner tarot course offered by a very kind and well-intentioned reader in the UK. He charged very minimally for a short collection of videos explaining each of the cards and their key meanings with a little numerology thrown in.

I was on my way.

What ensued after that course of learning was all up to me. I made a practice of studying and working with my cards on a daily basis, journaling, scrapbooking and absorbing all I could through research, familiarisation and scheduling in time around all of my daily obligations and commitments.

Learning to read tarot cards is no different to learning anything else in life that you would like to master. It involves practice, study, practice……and then a lot more practice and study.

I am an avid reader of books yet living with three visual learners I have, over time, realised that there are much more simple ways of gathering and retaining information other than solely through reading. My youngest Son would struggle with books even though his desire to read them was immense. He would collect books, smell the paper, look at the pages and then they would sit on the shelf. His passion was real but unfortunately, Dyslexia got in the way. Once, when he had to read something for school, I found him taking photos of the pages and then reading the pages through the photos on his phone.

This led me to contemplating what it would take for one of my own young adults to attempt to study the tarot cards and that was when I discovered the real lack of guidance out there for those who learn more by combining both images and words to assist them in retaining information.

I have written this book for all those beginners needing a place to start and also as a handy reference guide for the many of us currently practicing and reading tarot but who, every now and then, go blank. Place this book on your desk or bookshelf and use it to open your mind to the meanings, and also to the relationship between the cards in your spreads.

Newcomers to tarot are often hesitant to be open, or to announce their decision to learn and I can relate to this as I felt that way too. Some may not have the time or money to attend courses or even to follow an online program. Quietly, yet ambitiously, obtaining your first deck and book and studying at your own pace may be your approach, as was mine. If you have bought, or been given this book for that purpose, I encourage you to keep it in an accessible place so that when you have some spare time, or dedicated study periods, you can apply the meanings with your practice, developing and expanding them, as I will explain later on.

This book has photos of all the seventy-eight cards from the Rider Waite deck and as a quick and easy reference guide, those images have as many key terms as possible printed around the imagery, facilitating your learning and absorption of those meanings. Each suit has its imagery and captions presented on a coloured background to assist the visual learner. It is proven to be easier to absorb the information this way. The Major Arcana and the four suits will be colour coded for quicker referencing (print version only).

There is also a section on reversals with the same 'at a glance' key meanings, just so you have everything in one handy 'go to' manual.

My main aim in writing this book is to provide those images and key meanings so that when you have your deck in front of you a relationship is created. I will also cover a selection of topics related to the tarot and provide some of the most frequently asked questions and answers as posed by beginners everywhere.

I will try to keep my writing in this book simple and easy to read so that both your reading and learning time are an enjoyable experience giving you more time with your cards and less time struggling through lots of words.

We call our tarot cards our tools. They are the equipment from which we gain invaluable guidance, both when reading for ourselves and for others. I would like you to think of this book in the same way and refer to it as often as is needed for you to identify each card.

Let's begin your journey now.

Getting Started

"Start the way you want to finish"

I've always been a believer in this little saying. It definitely saves a lot of time and confusion down the track having a plan and a system in place to get you to where you want to be. In this case, a tarot reader.

To begin your studies using this book I would highly suggest that you purchase the **Rider Waite Tarot deck**. It is the highest selling tarot deck for a reason. I prefer not to go into the history of the tarot too much because that is not what this book is designed for and it is not my area of expertise. There are many good books covering the history written by very passionate people, so if you would like to delve into this, I suggest that you do further research in that area.

The Rider Waite deck was first produced in 1910 and is rich in the symbolism that we have come to associate with reading tarot. It is where our key meanings have evolved and been enriched over the years. The cards are essentially used for divination, which is the knowledge, guidance or outcomes predicted, based on taking the advice of the cards and trusting this information to have come from a divine source.

This deck is the most commonly used deck to commence studying with. Once you have become familiar with the images of the Rider Waite cards and their associated key meanings you will then be equipped to try your hand at reading with many of the other beautiful decks that are available to you. Who knows, one day you may even create a deck of your own. Get it right now and your options for the future are endless. Tarot is becoming an increasingly popular, and valued tradition in the lives of many people. The stigma attached to it is slowly giving way to it being welcomed and appreciated for the beneficial effects it can have on our lives, relationships, business and career matters.

With that deck, and this book in your hands you are ready to start on the wonderful journey of learning to read tarot. Yes, it is that simple. These are your tools. Use the notes section provided for each card or an additional journal or notebook to record your insights along the way.

You are set up and ready to go.

0 - Fool

Follow you heart

Seize the day

Thoughtlessness

Risk taking   A fall   Fun

Carefree

Trust in the Universe

Passion

Joker

Innocence

Travelling Lightly

Eccentricity

Freedom

Optimism

Free will

Foolish

Spontaneity

New adventures

Joker

Unlimited possibilities

Day dreaming

Improved health

Change of career   Getting a pet

Head in the clouds

New chapter   Rash decisions

Crazy in love

Trusting your intuition

End of troubles

The Fool

The Fool depicts someone who is obviously feeling a sense of freedom with little concern for material possessions, only carrying a small satchel. His gaze is directed towards the future disregarding any obstacles that may hinder his progress. The Sun, a representation of freedom, is shining brightly. At his side is his loyal companion, a little dog obviously warning of the danger in his master's steps.

This card lets us know that often in life we are presented with situations that may require us to take a 'leap of faith', take a risk, move ahead, with only an inner belief or intuitive 'knowing' to go by. It illustrates the innocence and childlike qualities of those who forget about consequences and act without thinking.

It can demonstrate the need to let go and bring more joy and fun into your life. The fool in a reading can identify new beginnings free from previous hardship, taking a new direction in life, opening up your mind to new ideas, plans and thoughts, while trusting in yourself, and your abilities.

Depending on where it falls in a spread it can also expose risky behaviour, being accident prone, failure to plan or being foolish.

Notes

The Magician - 1

Motivation to achieve

Self belief

Multi-tasking

Manifesting

Will power

Strength and determination

Making it happen

Creativity

Self confidence

Achieving goals

Originality

Talented

Problem solving

Trickster

Having vision

Magic

Being inspired to act

Getting the job done

Turning dreams into reality

Having a light bulb moment

The Magician

We see here a figure dressed in a red robe symbolising power and passion. He holds a double ended wand in one hand pointing to the heavens and his other free hand points to the earth. He stands in front of a table displaying tools representing the four elements, being his assistants in magic making. He has red roses above him and more roses and lilies at his feet. These flowers symbolise love and purity, success and happiness. He has an infinity symbol above his head depicting balance.

This card illustrates the possibility of turning one's thoughts and ideas into something real and tangible. It is a reminder that anything is possible to achieve, if you put your mind to it. A card of creation, and knowing that you have the ability, and the resources to make your dreams come true.

This is a card that affirms your focus and determination to succeed. It can be a card of action, will power, creativity, motivation, intention, talent and innovation.

Notes

The High Priestess - 2

Inner knowing

Reflection

Spirituality

Stillness

Patience

Having empathy

Trust in the process

Yoga teacher

Meditation

Inner wisdom

Guardian

Tarot reader

Psychic ability

Intuition

Acknowledging fears

Detecting insincerity

Quiet achiever

Secrecy

The High Priestess

A woman in a blue robes sits between two pillars, one marked 'B', the other marked 'J', supposedly representing dual polarities or opposing forces, This woman is a symbol of our spiritual side, identifying the need to trust our inner knowing, and indicating the need for balance in both action and inaction. She reminds us that at times it is necessary to trust and allow matters to evolve as they will without our physical interference.

This card asks us to be aware of the mysteries of life and encourages a belief in higher powers and the energy and benefits of trusting in the Universe.

We are also reminded through this card of our shadow side. The side of us that feeds our fears and insecurities. Trust in our inner voice is required when this card appears.

Notes

The Empress - 3

Mother figure
Nurturing
Abundance
Business success

Femininity

Sensuality

Fertility

Self care

Creativity

Pregnancy

Being grounded

Caring for others

Compassion

Support

Comfort

Nanny

Empathy

Matriarch

Security

Nurse or nursing
Spending time in nature

The Empress

The Empress sits on a red cushioned throne, or large chair, and wears a crown of twelve stars. She appears to be pregnant and her gown is covered in red roses symbolising love. She is backlit with a bright golden sky and has wheat growing at her feet.

All of this symbolism alludes to her representation of being the Mother of abundance, growth, success and security. This card can represent those aspects of either a person or a situation.

Any aspects of mothering, nurturing, care, compassion and nourishment are highlighted if this card appears. It can also indicate abundance and luxury, extravagance or feelings of richness.

There is also the suggestion of earthly and natural harmony within this card, given her outdoor environment and the harvest at her feet.

Notes

The Emperor - 4

Firmness

Control freak   Leader

Lives by rules

Wisdom

Highly moral

Manager

Stability

Fairness

Strength

Maturity

Self control

Father figure

Tolerance

Discipline

Bank manager

Boundaries

School Principle   Mediator

The Emperor

The image on this card depicts a very powerful looking man of authority sitting on a throne and demonstrating a sternness and firm standing.

If this card appears, it usually indicates a person with high values and a respect for law, order and structure. He sets a standard of behaviour that he enforces regimentally.

He can often represent a father figure, being a protector and leading by the highest of standards. He will take his role very seriously, whatever area that may be in, and have the utmost respect for rules and regulations.

The presence of the Emperor in a reading can be an indication of acting within the law, feeling confined or restrained, and also indicating fairness, reliability and power.

Notes

The Hierophant - 5

Tradition

Club

Conventional methods

Structure

Counsellor

Teacher

Therapist

Official

Hierarchy

Group learning

Hospital

Religion or Church

Priest or Pope

Confession

Sacraments

Organisational institutions

Conservative environment or person

Joining a gym group   Wedding

The Hierophant

The Hierophant shows a religious figure, sometimes thought of as a Pope, seated between two pillars with one hand holding a staff and the other raised in a sign of benediction, or blessing. Two priests are seen at the foot of the Hierophant, their gaze fixed on him and his actions.

This card symbolises the sharing of traditional values and faiths, either cultural or religious, in a disciplined manner.

It can also indicate the joining of a group or organisation that has a structured routine or regime. The Hierophant card can indicate an institution such as a hospital, bank, school, or any large group setting or environment.

Establishing routines and taking a traditional approach could be the message of this card. Joining a Gymnasium, Yoga class, language school, or any such modern establishment that operates under guidelines, may be another indication.

Notes

The Lovers - 6

Intimacy
Soul mate
Strong bond
Strong mutual attraction
Baring all
Mutual empowerment
Moral choices
Life choices
Sexual attraction
Relationships
Arranged marriage
Marriage
Authenticity
Choose wisely
Temptation
Crossroads
Developing individual beliefs
Successful business relationships
Possible infidelity

The Lovers

The lovers card seems quite straight forward showing a woman and a man reaching out to each other with the blessing and protection of an Angel above them, beneath a beautifully sunlit sky.

This card demonstrates love and the union of two people. It signifies commitment, connections, soul mates, intimacy and physical attraction.

It can also allude to the temptations and the moral and ethical choices we must make in life and within relationships.

When this card appears, it can remind us that if we make the right decisions and choices in any important areas of our lives, we can benefit greatly.

Notes

The Chariot - 7

Action Journey

Chauffer Competitive Confidence

Control Getting the job done

Will power Winning

Determination Race

Horse Races Car races

Driver Jockey

Motion Moving forward

Winning at all costs Success

Overnight success Swift action Focus and commitment

Uber driver or Uber ride

The Chariot

Within this card we see a princely figure in a chariot led by two Sphinxes, one black and one white. Although the Sphinxes are both stationary, the prince is ready for action looking confident and determined.

This is a card about winning, being successful and having the courage and dedication to overcome obstacles. Focus is recommended by appearance of the Chariot.

There is a double meaning within this card which is to be driven as a means of transportation, and also to be mentally driven to succeed.

Notes

Strength - 8

Growing strength

Inner strength

Bravery

Showing kindness

Reliability

Staying calm

Patience

Dog training

Raising children

Being persuasive

Influencer

Endurance

Control

Mediation

Human resources   Customer relations

Improved health

Offering comfort

Strength

Within the Strength card we see a woman in the presence of a lion. She has an infinity symbol over her head letting us know that she is balanced and in harmony with her surroundings. Her ability to gently but firmly manage the lion at her side is the heart of this card.

In a reading this card emphasises the need for patience at times, demonstrating tolerance and empathy for others, yet being firm and focused in your efforts.

If there is a particular issue where there may be doubt, the appearance of the Strength card is a wonderful reminder that you do have what it takes to persevere and succeed.

Notes

The Hermit - 9

Inner wisdom The need to understand

Thinking things over Inner knowing

Teacher

Change of direction

Mentor

Professor

Solitude

Isolation

Seeing the light

Time out

Introspection Seeking answers

Guidance Therapist

Discovery

Highlighting an issue

Shining a light on something

The Hermit

The Hermit card has the figure of an older man dressed in grey robes, holding a staff and carrying a lantern to light the path ahead of him.

The theme of this card is solitude. It lets us know that at times we need to take some time out for introspection. In busy times it can be overwhelming to find the solutions needed, so by quieting the mind, or getting away from it all, the answers are more likely to appear. Trusting your inner wisdom and having confidence in your own knowledge are highlighted by this card.

The Hermit card can identify the need to see a counsellor, teacher or seek the services of a professional.

Notes

Wheel of Fortune - 10

Change in circumstances

Sudden changes

Unexpected step forward

Taking a chance

Chance events

Unexpected step backwards

Accidents

Good luck

Finding answers

Forced hand

Prize winning

Twist of fate

Life speeds up

Surprises

Leaving things to fate

Being out of control

Expect the unexpected

Wheel of Fortune

In this card we see the wheel of life with all four elements depicted on the card. It constantly spins, where it will stop, nobody knows. That is the main message of this card. It can represent sudden changes in any direction in life. I often say when this card appears, "Expect the unexpected".

It can be an omen of good luck and confirmation that positive changes are on their way. There are often surprises in store and situations can take a turn in any direction.

The appearance of the Wheel of Fortune may also predict a broadening of your outlook due to a sudden change of events or your own mind set. Be open to the endless possibilities this card might be alluding to.

Notes

Justice - 11

Just actions

Fairness   Balance

                                Legal matters

Lawyer

                                Weighing things up

Confessing

                                Karma

Seeing the truth

                                Non judgemental

Taking responsibility

                                Punishment

Cause and effect

                                Correcting mistakes

Verdict

Settling disputes   Accountability

        Accepting consequences   Doing the right thing

Balanced outcome
        Repayment of debt

Justice

When looking at this card I am first drawn to the set of evenly balanced scales in one hand of the seated woman, along with a sword in the other hand. This indicates the need for a balanced outcome at all costs. The use of red as a dominant colour lets us know that power and strength emphasise and reinforce the key meaning. The half circle of yellow at the top of the card hints at a positive result should just actions be taken.

The requirement for justice can be seen as relevant in any reading regarding legal or ethical concerns. It can depict a person within the legal profession, or appear as an outcome, or motive for legal proceedings.

The Justice card also suggests Karma and the need to take responsibility for our behaviour. For every action, there is a reaction, every cause has an effect, and this card will highlight the importance of being accountable.

Notes

The Hanged Man - 12

Releasing control

Waiting for results

Change of mind

Leaving things be

Giving up

Alternative methods

Accepting progression

Taking a step back

New discoveries

Indecision

Waiting game

Avoiding arguments

'Light bulb' moment

Sacrifice

Letting go

Staying out of trouble

Seeing things from a different perspective

The Hanged Man

A young man hangs upside down from a tree by one leg, the other folded behind him. His arms are placed behind his back and he hangs in a rather relaxed state. He has a halo of golden light around his head which to me, indicates the necessity to see life from another perspective, allowing yourself to be open minded and receptive to change or alternative options.

You will notice that there is very little going on in the background of this card. Apart from the tree, we see a particularly empty space. I find this to be intentional as The Hanged Man suggests a time of pausing, and the release of control when necessary. Sometimes having faith in the Universe and allowing life to unfold as part of a grand plan is necessary when you have done your best but feel you may have run out of options.

This card can also indicate a time of sacrifice. You may have to put something on hold for the benefit of others, or in certain scenarios, go through tough times to achieve a goal or objective.

Notes

Death - 13

Transition   Unavoidable disturbances

Hand of fate

Confrontation   Renewal

Time for change   Change of attitude

End of an era   Clearing the air

Forced endings   Eliminating the unnecessary

Endings that create change

Inevitable event

Advancement through adversity

Letting go of toxic situations or people

Removing bad habits

Death

The Death card is possibly one of the most sinister looking cards in the Rider Waite Smith deck and that is unfortunate as its meaning is often misconstrued not only by the image, but also by its title. It depicts a black clad and skeletal horseman atop a white horse. At his feet are dead or dying people of all ages with a Pope giving out last rights.

The theme of this card is less likely to be related to a physical death, but more inclined to indicate changes around us which are involuntary but necessary for our future wellbeing. It is often through fear, lack of either motivation or prioritisation, that we hold onto many circumstances no longer serving us.

Enter the Death card, producing an unwanted occurrence, or major and inescapable change sent by the Universe for your ultimate benefit. When you see this card there is no need to be fearful. Your best interests are being brought forward for your attention and action. There may be a transition period necessary involving an extra amount of effort on your part, but retrospectively it will have been worth it.

Notes

Temperance - 14

Balance
Harmony
Compromising   Security
Flow
Moderation
Healing
Synchronicity
Good health
Recovery
Wellness
Meditation
Guardian angel
Reborn
Good natured
Replenishing
Peace

Balanced relationship
Being centred and calm

Temperance

Temperance appears when all is well and balanced in life. The image on the card is of an Angel with one foot in the water and one on land symbolising the balance of both our material, health and emotional wellbeing. The Angel wings are open and encompassing, often reminding us that we are protected at all times. The Sun rises in the background and all is well.

This card can represent the theory of everything in moderation, avoiding excess and overindulgence. Health and emotional strength can be indicated by the appearance of Temperance with harmony and balance achieved around you.

Notes

The Devil - 15

Addition Being materialistic

Feeling bound

Obsession

Bad mood

Overindulging

Jealousy

Hopelessness

Temptation

Superficiality

Con man

Loss of independence

Negativity

Being submissive

Lack of spirituality

Narrow mindedness Ignorance

Negative thought patterns

The Devil

The Devil card is another intimidating card within the Rider Waite Smith deck. The images exist to awaken our intuition and allow us to see, at a glance, the messages within. We have a devilish looking ogre enslaving both a male and a female figure. It couldn't be clearer!

What are you a slave to? Is it an addiction, a focus on material possessions, being tied down by controlling or manipulative individuals? Is your Employer working you to the bone? Are you more focused on the physical appearance of a person rather than focusing on their inner attributes? Have you lost your way spiritually because life has been so demanding?

These are all questions that you need to ask yourself when the Devil card appears. This card is not here to scare us....Or is it?

Notes

The Tower - 16

Disruptions   Sudden changes

Rebuilding

Panic   Crisis

Disaster   Release

Outburst

Losing

Confrontation

Argument

Major losses

Accident

Fire

Earthquake   Shock

Natural disaster   Explosion

Harsh discovery   Relationship breakdown

Unpleasant surprise   Terrorism

The Tower

If you thought the Devil card was confronting, the Tower card removes all doubt and adds another level of fear. I can say this knowing that, through my research, the Tower is the most feared card in the Tarot deck, no matter who the artist is. We have a tower collapsing in this image, with people being flung to the ground from the force of the destruction. It has never scared me personally, because I see it exactly as it is.

Look closely and you will discover that we are being shown a round roof that was never constructed to fit on a square structure. This is the basis of the key meaning of the Tower card. Whatever was established in your life without a solid foundation, would eventually fall apart. This can be a long and drawn out process for some and all those niggling doubts are confirmed in one explosive confrontation.

With my positive attitude, I am never scared of this card appearing in a reading. To me, although I realise that there will be an uncomfortable time looming, I see that whatever is changing will do so for my greater good. I will be released from something that held no security in the long term.

Notes

The Star - 17

Silver lining   Hope   Positive outlook

                                    Excitement
Faith

Anticipation   Motivation

                                    Kindness
Generosity

                                    All is well
Having a good day

                                    Peace of mind
Security

Pleasant encounter   Peace

Good news   Positive outcome

Inspiration   Feeling blessed

                          Light at the end of the tunnel
        Gratitude   Ideas

The Star

The Star card reveals a naked woman obviously experiencing the freedom of being unencumbered by the need for clothing. She is on bended knee at the water's edge, with one foot in the water and one on the land. The woman has two vessels in her hands. She pours water both into the lake, and onto the land beside her. Stars shine all around her, one quite brilliantly.

The Star card is suggestive of hope and faith. All ideas begin with hope. Without it there is no real will to succeed. Faith is having an expectation of a successful outcome and having the vision to know that anything is possible.

This card can also demonstrate generosity and warm heartedness. Giving of yourself in the hope of improving the lives of others.

It is an inspirational card to have appear in a reading letting you know that all can be well in any situation and asks that you have hope and faith.

Notes

The Moon - 18

Fear　　　　　Illusion

Overactive imagination
　　　　　　　Deceit

　　　　　　　　　　Worry
Anxiety

　　　　　　　Feeling isolated
Deception

Exaggeration　　　　Phobias

Confusion　　　　Being disillusioned

Shadow side
　　　　　　　Lack of courage

Weakness

　　　　　　　Schizophrenia
　　Vivid dreams

Lack of direction

　　　　　　　Disorientation

The Moon

Here we see a full moon shining brightly Within that full moon appears a crescent moon shaped face in profile, looking down on the earth below. A crayfish is seen climbing the banks of a river to gaze at the moon alongside a dog and a wolf.

Although, not a dark and sombre background, we are aware that the light of the moon can cast larger than life shadows, distorting the extent of any fears or worries, making them appear worse than they really are. It can be a card of warning alerting you to insincerity, deception or false friends.

It may also point to feelings of confusion, anxiety and stress. Often our worries can seem magnified at night which is what this card might indicate.

I will sometimes see this card appear as a way of determining the timing within a question. If it bears no meaning otherwise in a reading then it could be identifying an event, on or around, a full moon.

Notes

The Sun - 19

Freedom

Centre of attention

Vitality

Reborn

Success

Warm climate

Prize winner

Highly charged

Energised

Optimum health

Motivation

Being a shining light

Enjoying prosperity

Excitement

Joy of living

Fun

Achieving notoriety

Exposing the truth

Confidence

Enthusiasm

The Sun

A vibrant card in its expanse of yellow, the Sun shows a naked baby riding a horse and flying a large banner. Above the child is a blazing sun and behind, plantings of sunflowers bloom brightly.

This a wonderful card to have appear in any reading as contains so much positivity. If illness has been experienced, it can be an indicator of good health. Having the Sun show up lets you know a full recovery is imminent. Feeling an extra boost of energy and vitality are possible.

The Sun may be an indicator of travel, holidays or moving to a warmer climate. It can tell of freedom from restraints, being acknowledged or receiving accolades or awards.

Notes

Judgement - 20

Having an opinion

Representing a cause

Relief

Born again

Releasing guilt

Awakening

Brainstorming

Transformation

Confession

Fresh start

Paying dues

Punishment over

Redemption

Self worth

New ideas

Cleansing

Forgiveness

Making a difference

Putting the past behind you

Second chance

Making a judgement or being judged

Judgement

The Judgement card contains the image of a trumpet bearing Angel awakening the dead below who rejoice in their re-birth.

It tells of transformation and second chances, starting over and being given new opportunities. Where an injustice has occurred, it brings judgement and the need to make amends.

This is another positive card as a sign of forgiveness and having paid any dues, bringing a release of guilt or sorrow. It is also an indication of new areas of life that may be enticing or calling you.

Notes

The World - 21

Completion

New chapter

Goals realised

World travel

Unity

End of difficult times

Global issues

Serving others

Feeling satisfied

Gratitude

Having it all

Passport renewal

Working as a unit

Balance

Wholeness

Feelings of accomplishment

Finding solutions

Change of location

Humanitarian activities

Integration

The World

The World is the final card in the major arcana. Again, we have the nearly naked woman, symbolising freedom within a green wreath of success. Representation of the four elements are in each corner indicating harmony has been achieved.

If you now know the story of the Fool's journey, you will understand the significance of the World card in a reading. If hardships and challenges have plagued you, this card will mark a definite end to those troubling times.

If can be a card of transitioning to another stage in life's journey. It may also indicate the completion of any major projects or accomplishments of importance.

Notes

Ace of Wands

Creative beginning

Originality

New projects

Birth

Enthusiasm

Passionate pursuit

New business

Offer

Motivation

Proposal

Sales pitch

Confident attitude

Being adventurous

Potential

High self esteem

Being bold

Having optimism

Opportunity

Guaranteed success with effort

Taking on a challenge

Creating an action plan

Ace of Wands

The Ace of Wands shows a hand protruding from a cloud holding a wand or branch sprouting new green leaves. The background although quite neutral, displays a flourishing landscape.

The Aces in each suit have rather large images, and in my opinion, this is a significant indicator of the strength of the message within the card. The energies associated with the Wands suit are all available to you if this card comes up in a spread or reading. You are being offered an opportunity, a chance to begin something that could be of great importance, but as with any of the Aces, the hard work must be done by you if you wish to succeed.

The Ace of Wands indicates confidence in yourself and your ability to move forward. There may be an air of excitement around you and a sense of enthusiasm and motivation. New beginnings that require all of the above qualities may be present with the appearance of this card.

The Ace of wands can also represent a birth in any form.

Notes

Two of Wands

Planning

Preparation

Holding the world in your hands

Travel planning

Influencer

Goal setting

Moving forward

Pioneering

Showing initiative

Invention

Being daring

Unique approach

Team leader

Tour guide

Championing a cause

Rising to the challenge

Party planner

Travel agent

Two of Wands

The Two of Wands depicts a man dressed in brown robes holding a globe of the world in his hands as he stands between two spouting rods, or wands, and looks out at the land below.

I instantly see this card as 'having the world in your hands'. Making the most of opportunities is the important message within. It is a card that encourages a leadership role and the development of plans and actions needed to achieve your goals. Good foundations are the basis of any concept, and your progress depends on your initiative and motivation.

Having the courage to speak your mind, or being actively involved in public speaking, may also be another aspect of the Two of Wands.

Notes

Three of Wands

Putting plans into action

Leadership

Taking on a new project

To set the wheels in motion

Planning for the future

Development

Postage

Sea cargo

Director

Promotion

Anticipation

Hiking

Brainstorming

Motivating others

Dispatch

Facing fears

Seeing the bigger picture

Leading by example

Setting the stage

Three of Wands

In this card we see a man in a red robe with a touch of yellow standing on the land but looking out to sea. He has three wands firmly planted around him and holds one as he stands there. In the distance his gaze, although we can't see it, looks to be directed at some ships sailing past.

The Three of Wands follows on from the previous card where foundations were laid. Plans may now be in the early stages of progress. This card is about leadership by example, providing guidance and structure for others to follow, and being responsible for the set up and implementation of programs or schemes.

It can also advise of the need to step outside of your comfort zone and try something new, be it travel, career or relationship changes.

Notes

Four of Wands

Celebrations

Milestone occasion

Wedding reception

Congratulations

Surprise party

Socialising

Excitement

Joy

House move

New home

Festival

Good news

Awards ceremony

Social gathering

Freedom

Competition win

Amicable divorce

High energy   Interior design

Four of Wands

The Four of Wands is a wonderful card of celebration and happiness. Two women are carrying flowers above their heads as they stand in front of a large building where others are congregating in the background. There are four wands framing this image and those wands are adorned with garlands of flowers.

This card highlights good times, celebrations, engagements or weddings, getting together with friends and any other happy and special occasions.

If this card comes up for you, be prepared for exciting times where the energy will be high and the mood, joyful.

Notes

Five of Wands

Competition

Arguments

Debating

Bullying

Lack of teamwork

Anxiety

Street fight

Sporting event

The need to win

Setbacks

Challenges

Disharmony

Lack of cohesion

Defence

Immature actions

Protest

Sulking

Childish behaviour

Being opinionated

Five of Wands

In this card, our wands are no longer upright and firmly planted but are being used in competitive tussle between five young men. Some are charging with their wands and others are using them in defence.

The suggestion of this card is one of disharmony and rivalry. It can indicate arguments, disagreements, debating, poor teamwork and lack of cohesion within a group. Expect some tension when you see this card if it appears in a troubled situation.

Sporting or any other competition or contest can also be indicated by the presence of the Five of Wands.

Notes

Six of wands

Proud moment

Success

Being popular

Good self-esteem

Being acknowledged

Recognition

Receiving praise

Having a big ego

Winning

Time to shine

Prize win

Receiving an award

Promotion

Centre of attention

Congratulations

Pride march

Holding your head high

Gloating

Job well done

Having a large following

Six of wands

The Six of Wands pictures a man wearing a wreath on his head, riding a horse while being cheered along by well-wishers all carrying their wands high in acclaim for the rider's victory. The horseman also has a wreath on his own wand.

This card points to personal satisfaction and public acknowledgement for your efforts in any area. It may be through praise, compliments, rewards, recognition or promotion. It may provide a short-term reward being a motivating force as you move forward with a goal or task.

The Six of wands can also indicate self-importance, moments of pride in yourself, and sometimes being a bit egotistical, or outwardly over-confident.

Notes

Seven of Wands

Gaining strength

Self defence

Fighting back

Being judged

Disorientation

Creating boundaries

Resistance

Facing fears

Gaining confidence

Staying on top of things

Being brave

Being stubborn

Exercising the right to say 'No'

Taking charge

Being firm

Putting up a good fight

Standing up for what you believe in

Refusing to be intimidated

Building a stronger immune system

Seven of Wands

In this card we see a young man using his wand in defence of six other wands all directed at him from below. His stance lets us know that he is defending or standing up for himself. He wears two different shoes which may hint at prior struggles and can also illustrate his instability.

This card can encourage you to rise above challenges or indicate that you indeed are. When faced with a difficult situation, you are reminded to stand up for what you believe in, hold your ground and defend yourself.

It can urge you to be firm in your actions and not be influenced by those of a lesser character. Another indication of the Seven of wands could be overcoming depression, addiction or lethargy and having the ability to continue moving forward to face even further challenges, with growing strength and stamina.

Notes

Eight of Wands

Overnight success

Changing the pace

Speeding

Swift action

Taking aim

Unexpected news

Travel by air

Exposing the truth

Hitting the mark

Archery

Resolutions

Action

Synchronisation

Highly motivated

Stepping up

Change

Moving on

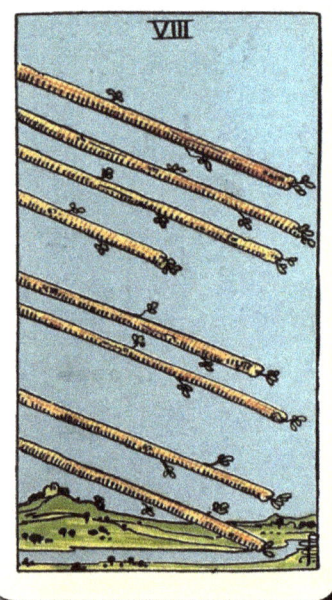

Successful business transaction

Jumping to conclusions

Running away

Eight of wands

The Eight of Wands, commonly considered one of the wish cards in the deck, has no image of a person within it, just the eight wands, obviously in motion, and all heading for the same target.

It speaks of swiftness in any context such as the receiving of important news, reaching a quick conclusion, getting to the heart of the matter and speeding up procedures or operations.

It can be a wonderful indication that you are not only on the right path, but also advancing with momentum. This card has a very high energy within the Wands suit and is always a good one to receive in a reading as confirmation of either timing or success.

Notes

Nine of Wands

Perseverance

Endurance

Stamina

Breaking down barriers

Being defensive

Determination

Overcoming adversity

Will power

Paranoia

Being wary

Long and drawn out recovery

Bad memories

Being protective

Lacking trust

Getting out of jail

Battling with inner demons

Struggling with anxiety

Light at the end of the tunnel

Nine of Wands

The Nine of Wands has a dishevelled looking man with a bandage on his head standing in front of a wall of eight wands. The wand he holds is the ninth wand and also the one removed by him to penetrate through to the other side. It is within this image that the message lies.

Difficult times have come before you. Those challenges have left their scars and although they are behind you, slight concern and insecurity is still felt. You may have had to defend yourself or something you stand for or represent, and that defensive attitude may have drained you.

It affirms that your perseverance has paid off through sheer will and determination. This card advises you to keep pushing forward as the end is in sight. Fatigue will fade with success and scars will heal over time.

Notes

Ten of Wands

- Heavy load
- Taking on too much
- Refusing to delegate
- Nearing the end
- Overtime
- Physically demanding work
- Back issues
- Overdoing it
- Extreme tiredness
- Going it alone
- Problem solving
- Taking on all the responsibility
- Being weighed down
- Assuming blame
- Worry
- Heavy lifting
- Meeting deadlines
- Experiencing guilt
- Acting the martyr

Ten of wands

The Ten of Wands image is that of a man heavily burdened by the load of wands he is carrying. He hunches forward due to the weight of his task. In the far distance, ahead of him, is his destination. Its distance is daunting yet provides an incentive to keep advancing.

This card reinforces that you may be feeling overburdened when it appears in a spread. You may be working overtime, taking on more than you can handle or doing more than your fair share.

There are many other explanations within this card such as boredom, being punished for shirking responsibility, feeling overwhelmed by obligations, or even health issues, such as a bad back.

The positive aspect of this ending card, numbered ten, is the reference to the house in the distance. Keep in mind that your issues are in their final stages.

Notes

Page of Wands

Influencer
Ambitious
Intern
Attractive
Motivated
Popular
Spirited
Up for a challenge
Fearless attitude
Risk taker
Life of the party
Inventive
Passionate
Adventurous
Likes to be the centre of attention
Likable
Excitable
Expressive
Playful   Optimistic

Page of Wands

The Page of Wands portrays a well to do young man wearing more extravagant robes with a feathered hat, confidently holding his wand in front of him and gazing up at it. The land around him is vast and barren but the sky is blue and bright.

This Page is full of untapped energy. He has the confidence before having the skill and is an example of the type of energy that may be required if he appears in a reading.

Creativity and natural talent could be suggested by this card and it is often associated with a younger age group that will have the courage, drive and ambition to have an impact in any situation.

He can express passionate pursuits and taking on new endeavours with motivation and charisma.

Notes

Knight of wands

Good looking

Positive attitude

Reckless

Hero

Gets the job done

Can take on too much

Showy

Extreme sports

Restless

Angers easily

Spontaneity

Charisma

Good news

Originality

Attention seeker

Progression

Energetic

High sex appeal

Lacking commitment

Disregard for consequences

Knight of wands

The Knight of Wands shows us a helmeted knight atop a rearing horse. He carries his wand with one hand while directing his horse with the other.

Action is indicated in this card and this action is with intent. It may represent an individual who has a goal and the determination to achieve it in any given situation. Even in a romance reading it can indicate being pursued.

Good news being delivered is another option with this card and spontaneity, originality, creativity and the spirit of adventure are all traits associated with the Knight of Wands.

As a person this card will represent someone sociable, charismatic and possibly flamboyant.

Notes

Queen of Wands

Sociable

High self esteem

Open minded

Attracts attention

Instinctive

Gets things done

Sincere & honest

Direct in communication

Sporty

Gym instructor

Athletics coach or leader

Confident

Highly optimistic

White Witch

Charismatic

Motivator

Outgoing personality

Constantly busy

Uplifts others

Queen of Wands

The Queen of Wands sits on a striking throne. Her gaze is a little off centre suggesting that her personality is that of an open minded individual. She has her wand in one hand and a blooming sunflower in the other. At her feet sits her scruffy black cat.

As an individual we are reminded of someone who is confident and comfortable within themselves. While possibly seeming a little egotistical, her charm and charisma make her attractive and likeable.

The cat at her feet can symbolise her possible interest in witchcraft and the supernatural. She trusts her own instincts and acts with positivity and determination.

This card can represent leadership qualities and a highly motivated person. Acting on beliefs and being a good entertainer are other attributes associated with the Queen of Wands.

Notes

King of Wands

Highly creative

Magnetic persona

Influential

Powerful & forceful

Assertive

Respected

Explorer

Able to handle a crisis

Highly creative

Eccentric

Motivating force

Inspirational leader

Confrontational

Flamboyant

Open to challenges

Passionate

Commanding presence

Entertainer

Stands out in a crowd

Performer

King of Wands

The King of Wands sits on his golden throne and gazes ahead with intent and purpose. He holds his wand in one hand while the other rests comfortably on his thigh. At his feet is a Salamander symbolising both passion and fire, which are common to the wands suit.

The King of Wands is a highly motivated and enthusiastic leader in any situation, be it in business, sporting or in a social environment. He inspires others with his communication and ingenuity. He can create a sense of excitement that has powerful consequences.

He is often outgoing and possibly flamboyant in nature and will usually be the initiator of social gatherings and events. Anyone associated with this card will be dominant, magnetic and open to challenges.

Notes

Ace of Pentacles

New job opportunity

Investing money

Bank loan approval

Alternative treatment

Prize money

Learning a new skill

Abundance

New lease of life

Promotion

Invention or idea

Tax refund

Landscaping a new garden

New home

Inheritance received

Finding effective medication

Ace of Pentacles

As it is with all the Aces, a rather large hand extends from a cloud and is holding a Pentacle in its palm. The sky is neutral, but the landscape is lush with a pathway leading through an arch of greenery, towards the mountains in the distance.

All of this symbolism represents the opportunity for practical growth in your life. A fresh start, or a new beginning, is available to you with the chance of realising your full potential, in a way that is tangible.

This possibility of abundance may be associated with career, assets, study, health or physical well being.

Whenever you see the Aces in a reading know that the opportunities are reliant on your input to become a realisation.

Notes

Two of Pentacles

Life work balance

Ability to adapt

Gaining momentum

Demanding conditions

Managing challenges

Smooth sailing

Flexibility

Proud of your accomplishments

Performer

Taking time out

Having fun

Switching from one task to another

Multi-tasking

Life of the party

Beach games

Maintaining balance

Job satisfaction

Going with the flow of life

Two of Pentacles

The Two of Pentacles shows a young man, wearing an unusually large hat and juggling two pentacles within an infinity symbol. He balances on one leg as if to demonstrate his ability to manage more than the average person. Behind him two ships stay afloat on rough seas. The young man's focus is on the pentacles in his hands.

The emphasis of this card is on the need for balance in life. Its focus is on managing all that is thrown at you, which is often when least expected. Change can be daunting, and when this card appears, you are encouraged to handle challenges by being mindful of each task and managing efficiently.

It can represent being overloaded or having to juggle or navigate through difficulties but can also indicate an enjoyment and satisfaction in being busy and doing something you love.

Notes

Three of Pentacles

Teamwork

Co-ordination

Quality workmanship

Artisan

Quality control

Workplace review

Working overtime

Contract signing

Preparation

Common goals

Craftsmanship

Home renovations

Group project

Health consultation

Doing what's expected

Professional consultation

Performance review

Project management

Working to a deadline

Three of Pentacles

The Three of Pentacles has three figures in its image. A tradesperson is working within an archway that has three pentacles inserted at its highest point. Two other people of authority are consulting with the tradesperson for the mutual benefit of all three and the validity of their project.

This card is a reminder of the need to work together harmoniously to produce the desired outcome. It indicates that planning, preparation and organisation are all key elements for success. The Three of Pentacles will often appear in the early stages of a project or enterprise.

Hard work, commitment and excellence are all characteristics of this card.

Notes

Four of Pentacles

Over controlling

Lack of control

Greed

Possessive

Inner city development

Hoarding

Stubbornness

Frugality

Resistance

Narrow mindedness

Doing it your way

Maintaining a health program

Sticking to a routine

Opposing development

Creating a structure

Resisting progress

Saving for a rainy day

Financial management

Putting all your eggs in one basket

Four of Pentacles

In this card we see a man sitting on a chest, presumably full of money. He has one pentacle in his hands, one on his head and he secures two with his feet. Behind him is a city symbolising development.

We usually associate this card with control. That can mean being possessive, greedy or materialistic, or alternatively it can be seen as having control over finances, creating order and being organised.

Depending on the context of the spread or reading this card can indicate a need to let go and allow a more natural development, or the need to spend money to make money. It might be a reminder to create a budget and be mindful of where your money is spent.

Notes

Five of Pentacles

Financial insecurity

Loss of income

Loneliness'

Outdated

Loss of job

Feeling ill

Feeling unsupported

Being excluded

Being rejected

Needing medical attention

Looking for charity

Being homeless

Being without heating

Being unpopular

Being ignored

Not taking care of yourself

Out of fashion

Unable to make ends meet

Being made redundant

Five of Pentacles

The Five of Pentacles is one of the cards in the deck that illustrates snow and emphasises the coldness within the image. Two wayward and forlorn figures dressed in rags and without shoes, walk through the snow, one with crutches, the other covering their head as protection from the cold. The stained-glass window alludes to a church or place of safety.

This card highlights insecurity and hardship. It can appear when experiencing financial troubles or loss, redundancy, loneliness or rejection. Sometimes, depending on the spread this card can indicate ill health or depression.

When this card appears in a reading, be reminded that there is always someone to lean on in life. You are supported.

Notes

Six of Pentacles

Charity
Giving
Pay day
Gratitude
Financial balance
Receiving
Assistance
Give and take
Sharing knowledge
Splitting the bill
Doing charity work
Busker
Breaking even
Charity event
Being humbled
Sharing winnings
Being rescued
Dominating
Roadside assistance
Offering advice
Profit and loss statement

Six of Pentacles

In the Six of Pentacles we see a well-dressed man carrying a balanced set of scales in one hand and with the other he hands out coins to one of two beggars kneeling at his feet. The six pentacle symbols frame the image overhead in an unbalanced pattern.

This card can suggest the need to give and take in life. There are times when you may be in a position to be generous, and other times where you may need assistance from others. It is often referred to as the card of charity.

It may also speak of financial balance, with enough money coming in to cover expenses and may also represent loan applications or refinancing.

In health matters it can suggest finding a healthy balance or receiving medication to suit your condition.

Notes

Seven of Pentacles

Stock take

Accountability

Evaluation

Time out

Reflection

Performance review

Annual review

Landscape gardener

Assessing investments

Tax return

Progress report

Internal audit

Bank statements

Health assessment

Rethinking the future

Looking for alternatives

Living off the land

Contemplating change

Pride in achievements

Seven of Pentacles

The Seven of Pentacles depicts a young worker leaning on his gardening tool and assessing the growth of his garden. The seven pentacles are his harvest, yet to be picked, and behind him we see water flowing before a mountainous backdrop.

This card is about evaluating and assessing your progress. It can highlight the need to pause and reflect on how far you have come with a task or project and make some adjustments for the future. It may also pinpoint the need for a break to clear the mind and rest the body.

I sometimes see this card as efforts being assessed. That may be in the form of a review within your workplace or it could be a financial assessment of some sort.

It can also indicate a time of completion and the desire to diversify or move on. This might apply to a career, home or a location change.

Notes

Eight of Pentacles

Apprenticeship
Working hard
Detailing
Craftsman
Further study
Diligence
Research
Training
Commitment
Focus
Using your talents
Good work ethic
Tying up loose ends
Production line
Attention to detail
Trophy display
Working outdoors
Dedication to a project
Applying effort and expertise
Collector

Eight of Pentacles

In the Eight of Pentacles a young man sits on a bench and works diligently on the pentacle in his hands. Six completed pentacles are displayed in front of him and one lays at his side.

This card reveals your commitment and dedication whenever it appears in a reading. Giving something your total attention and focus is indicated here and the application of knowledge and skill to any situation.

It can also indicate apprenticeships, been trained or mentored, the acquiring of new skills, and talents and research. It suggests a good work ethic and being dedicated to seeing something through to its completion.

This card may suggest furthering your education or adding to a resume or job application. It can also signify the completion of tax returns.

Notes

Nine of Pentacles

Discipline
Self-control
Luxury
Retirement
Getting outdoors
Day of Leisure
Living comfortably
Time out
A day at a Winery
Life's luxuries
Sommelier
Vineyard owner
Financial security
Self- made wealth
Refinement
Reward for effort
Well kept
Abundance
Fashionable
Self-reliance
Well spoken

Nine of Pentacles

The positivity of the Nine of Pentacles is emphasised by use of bright yellow in many aspects of this card. A well figured woman dressed luxuriously, relaxes in a thriving vineyard. On one gloved hand a bird perches, suggesting that she has time for hobbies and extravagant past times. Her righthand rests on a stack of pentacles with more pentacles to her left. In the background sits a stately home. The sun shines around her giving the impression that all is well in her world.

This is a wonderful card to appear in a reading as it illustrates the achievement of financial security in life at an age that allows you to enjoy the rewards for your efforts. It indicates self-reliance, being disciplined and controlled, and also having the ability to be comfortable with your own company.

It signifies an appreciation for life and what you have accomplished, enjoying both the material aspects, and also making the most of the experiences associated with financial success and abundance.

Notes

Ten of Pentacles

Inheritance
Retirement
Good fortune
Security
Financial success
Family gathering
Gated community
Upgrading the family home
Aged care
Pension
Grandparents
Routine actions
Cultural events
Traditions
Having it all
Wealth
Community event
Permanence
Long term health plan
Conservative attitude
Experiencing good health

Ten of Pentacles

Within the Ten of Pentacles we see an elderly well robed man sitting before an archway. He is surrounded by ten Pentacles. At his feet are two loyal dogs, and in front of him family members, both adult children and grandchildren, interact. Beyond the archway we see what we assume is the family home.

This card suggests retirement in a comfortable fashion. It speaks of family, abundance, inheritance, financial security, good fortune and the culmination of a successful life and career.

Upgrading the family home can be another interpretation of this card as well as retirement or aged care. In answer to any long-term plans, the appearance of this card would highly illustrate that you are on the right track and it is an encouraging card to receive.

Notes

Page of Pentacles

Study

Desire to be successful

Striving for financial security

Internship

Being reliable

Assistant manager

First pay cheque

First job

Managing money more effectively

Class captain

Being mentored

Good news

Coping in the real world

Mature young person

Graduation

Setting goals

Taking on responsibility

Dependable

Working to change something

Page of Pentacles

In this card we see a young man practically clothed, holding up, and gazing at a Pentacle. He holds the Pentacle quite reverently realising its worth. Golden sunlight, a lush landscape and flowing water surround him.

This Page is learning the effectiveness and the value of hard work. He takes a positive and practical approach to his study and learning, knowing that his attitude and work ethic will reward him in the long term.

He has the foresight to see that the determination and strength he displays now will give him the stability and security he wants in the future.

This card depicts dependability, trustworthiness and learning in a traditional way.

Notes

Knight of Pentacles

Dependable

Consistency

Likes routine

Hard working

Relentless

Obsessive

Perfectionist

Thorough

Forward thinking

Can be inflexible

Cautious

Taking commitments seriously

Traditional beliefs

Conservative

Fear of taking risks

Attention to detail

Uses trusted methodology

Sometimes pessimistic

Knight of Pentacles

The Knight of Pentacles shows a man in armour sitting on a stationary horse. He holds his Pentacle reverently in his hands, as does the page, with no need to hold the reigns of his horse. There is bright golden light around him suggesting prosperity.

This Knight advises of the need to act carefully, cautiously and with methods that are proven to be efficient. He suggests the need to be practical and thorough always covering every aspect of a situation and completing every task consistently. He can have strong ingrained traditional beliefs and firmly defend those ideals.

The negative aspects of this card can include stubbornness, inflexibility, pessimism, lack of spontaneity and fear of taking risks.

Notes

Queen of Pentacles

Practical

Nurturing

Generous

Hospitable

Is loving and supportive

Demonstrates reliability

Offers security

Animal lover

Honest

Uses logic

Demonstrates loyalty

Is patient

Offers praise

Resourceful

Can be a good gardener

Good with children

Can find a use for anything

Welcoming nature

Creates structure & routine

Queen of Pentacles

In this card we see a sensibly robed Queen with a modest crown sitting on her throne, gazing adoringly at the Pentacle she holds in her lap. She is surrounded by blooming flowers overhead and a lush garden. Flowing water and low-lying mountains are visible in the background. A rabbit scurries past her symbolising fertility and abundance.

The Queen of wands can depict a person who is reliable and dependable. This person's success has been achieved through dedication and hard work. They can always be relied upon to be both supportive, resourceful, helpful, warm and welcoming. They may be known for their hospitality and generosity.

Usually confident and successful, they do not portray this but act modestly and in a humble and grateful manner. As a friend or partner, there will be none more loyal than the Queen of Pentacles.

Notes

King of Pentacles

Successful   Opportunist

       Self-employed

Has the Midas touch   Persistent

                       Business Person

Bank Manager

                       Motivates others

Competent

                       Natural leader

Thick skinned

                       Thrives on routine

Always available

                       Self- confident

People manager

                       Quick thinker

Skilled at delegating   Remains calm in a crisis

Will stop at nothing to achieve a goal

King of Pentacles

The King of Pentacles sits on his elaborate throne dressed for success and quite proud of his position. He holds a sceptre in one hand and confidently displays his Pentacle with the other. The garden that surrounds him is not modest but grows abundantly and vigorously. Behind him his estate can be seen standing tall and solid.

This king is very proud of his accomplishments and is not afraid to announce it. His hard work ethic and determined nature allow him to be recognised and appreciated. His successes are his business card, and as a person in a reading or spread, you can be sure that wealth and accumulated wisdom, security and a reliable reputation have been realised.

This card can represent a Father figure, manager, businessperson, or anyone with authority and integrity.

Notes

Ace of Cups

New love

Being empathetic

Following your intuition

Feeling better

First kiss

Making new friends

Forgiveness

Receiving a gift

Releasing negativity

Offering support

Offer

Birth

An offer of support

Loving message

Feeling loved

Honeymoon

Getting a pet

Following your heart

Butterflies in the stomach

Emotional connection

Psychic development

Ace of Cups

The Ace of Cups has a chalice held in the palm of a hand that protrudes from a cloud, suggesting that it is sent from the Divine. Water flows from the chalice like a fountain, and a dove of peace casts a sacred sacrament into the cup. Droplets of water fall lightly down from the chalice representing the emotion of feelings. Water lilies float peacefully in a lake below.

This Ace offers the opportunity of emotional fulfilment, joy and happiness. It lets you know that your heart may be opened to new feelings be they through romance, relationships, intuition or any other change that is for your emotional and mental wellbeing.

The appearance of this card may indicate the release or letting go of negative or toxic people or situations that may have held you back or caused distress. Alternatively, it can signal a new relationship, holding the promise of being a soul connection, either romantic or otherwise.

Notes

Two of Cups

Soul mate

Handshake agreement

Falling in love

Anniversary

Best friend

Sharing

Forgiveness

Truce

Physical attraction

Bonding

Partnership

Ceremony

Wedding

Making amends

Out for drinks

Seeing a practitioner

Having things in common

Making a connection

Emotional attraction

Two of Cups

In the Two of Cups a man and a woman face each other and exchange cups. This can represent an agreement or consolidation, a truce or traditional ceremony. Above them, the winged lion validates the union. They stand on, what looks to be a platform, above a lush and green landscape and blue skies.

When the Two of Cups appears, it can suggest a strong connection as in a soul mate, marriage, friendship and sharing common goals or objectives.

It can also indicate a business partnership or arrangement and possibly, the signing of contracts or a 'hand-shake' deal.

The Two of Cups can also relate to forgiveness, or making amends, following a disagreement.

Notes

Three of Cups

Dancing
Street party
Feelings of excitement
Celebrations
Getting out
Letting your hair down
Support group
Having things in common
Raising a glass
Harvesting
Teamwork
Team motivator
Music festival
Bridal party
Hospitality
Birthday party
Happy hour

Girls night out
Boys night out

Community spirit

Three of Cups

In the Three of Cups three women are seen forming a circle and joyfully dancing while they raise their glasses, or cups in celebration. The women wear wreaths of flowers in their hair and feast on fruit and the harvest that is at their feet.

This card may appear when congratulations are in order. It is a high energy card and instantly stirs a sense of happiness and excitement.

It can represent any kind of gathering for pleasure, fun and togetherness. Social occasions and milestone events can be indicated by this card.

The Three of Cups can also signify support groups, getting together with others for a common cause or interest and close friendships.

Notes

Four of Cups

Rejection

Multiple choices

Being self-absorbed

Missing out

Sulking

Missed opportunity

Having too many options

Lacking motivation

Procrastinating

Being guarded

Being reclusive

Playing Poker

Meditation

Yoga

Being stubborn

Not listening

Taking things too seriously

Being indecisive

Withdrawal

Rejection

Playing hard to get

Four of Cups

In the Four of Cups we see a young man sitting cross legged beneath a tree with his arms folded. In front of him three cups have been placed in a row and a fourth cup is being offered from a hand that appears in the atmosphere beside him.

This card can indicate the frustration of having too many options, or issues to deal with and not trusting our intuition to guide us.

It can also represent worry, fear, self-absorption and being closed minded or shut off from reality. It may highlight a time of feeling down or unmotivated and the need for some time out.

It can also emphasise the need for meditation and solitude to obtain a clearer perspective.

Notes

Five of Cups

Depression

Grief

Loss

Giving up

Despair

Crying over spilt milk

Crying

Lethargy

Heartache

Bereavement

Lack of brightness

Losing

Emotional pain

The need for gratitude

Sadness

Making a costly mistake

The need for recovery

Regret for what might have been

Try to look on the bright side

The need to focus on what you have, not what is lacking

Five of Cups

In the Five of Cups a man stands before three fallen cups, spilling their contents at his feet. We can see both red and clear liquid on the ground and to me, that signifies blood and tears. He also has two upright cups behind him, but his body language suggests that he doesn't have the energy or desire to notice them. The sky is grey reflecting further heaviness in the message of this card. A river flows between the man and the dwelling in the distance.

This card immediately suggests depression and the inability to see any light or brightness. It epitomises bereavement, loss, grief and heartache.

The Five of Cups can be representative of any occasion that causes emotional pain or regret. The message of this card is that there is always hope, and the ability to work with whatever is at hand, to trust in the power of the human spirit and see the light at the end of the tunnel.

Notes

Six of Cups

Security

Nostalgia

Giving

Generosity

Being the bigger person

Reminiscing

Fun and games

Having a good attitude

Act of kindness

Childcare

Sharing

Protection

After school care

Gift giving

Nursery

Memories

Raising children

Feeling light-hearted

Innocence

Taking time out to smell the roses

Six of Cups

In the Six of Cups we see two children, one quite a bit larger than the other, signifying the act of being the 'bigger person'. The taller child extends a large pot of flowers to the smaller child. The two appear to be in a gated community, or garden, and are surrounded by flowers. There is a sense of security present in this card.

This card embodies the gesture of generosity and gift giving. It is also a reminder of childhood and the familiar events that took place in years gone by. It can be a card of nostalgia and reminiscing.

The Six of Cups may indicate sharing and the act of kindness. It might also represent feelings of security, safety and being protected.

Notes

Seven of Cups

Wishful thinking

Choices

Appearances can be deceiving

Procrastination

Day dreaming

Hallucinating

False dreams

Good imagination

Lack of commitment

Emotional rollercoaster

Mental breakdown

Mind games

Weighing up options

Overactive mind

Excessiveness

Be careful what you wish for

Keeping your options open

Not living in reality

Seven of Cups

The Seven of Cups has the silhouette of a man with his back to us looking at seven cups filled to overflowing with various options or choices. We have symbolism of many different desires and fears of the human mind, all floating on a cloud suggesting that imagination and thought is involved in this process. There are symbols of love, fear, material possessions and ego all there for the choosing.

It is known as the card of 'wishful thinking' and often sends the message in a reading to be careful what you wish for. It can reflect an overactive imagination and the need to be realistic.

This card can often suggest the need to be careful when making important decisions. What may appear to be attractive may have hidden aspects of a negative nature, and alternatively, that which is not so attractive, may be the more sure and safe option.

The Seven of Cups can also represent daydreaming and procrastination.

Notes

Eight of Cups

Walking away

Something missing from life

Saying goodbye

Time to move on

Better ahead

Removing yourself from a toxic situation

Fighting fear

Hiking

Emotional breakdown

Exhaustion

Hopelessness

Divorce

Relocation

End of lease

Uphill battle

Lethargy

Leaving home

Emotionally drained

Leaving an unsatisfying job

Taking your power back

Eight of Cups

The Eight of Cups shows a man in a red cape walking away from the cups he has so carefully tended to. He walks by the light of a full moon and has an uphill climb away from the water that flows around him. There is no suggestion of vegetation or growth where his cups are placed, but he moves forward on greener ground.

This card symbolises walking away from whatever no longer serves you emotionally. The fact that there is one obvious space left between the cups, leads to the belief that something was missing, or lacking in the situation.

The green grass beneath his feet may suggest that there are better times ahead than are left behind.

If this card appears in a reading it can be a sign that it is time to move on as there is no more that can be done in your current environment. It signifies being emotionally spent and knowing that walking away is in your best interests.

Notes

Nine of Cups

Emotional satisfaction

Having it all

Achieving a goal

High self-esteem

Feeling loving

Feelings of contentment

Appreciating luxury

Appreciating beauty

Realising a dream

Dining experience

Collector or collection

Art collector

Feeling smug

Inner peace

Falling in love

Getting your wish

Doing it your way

Drinking someone under the table

Nine of Cups

The Nine of Cups shows a man wearing a red hat, the colour of success and passion. He sits on a stool in front of an elaborate display of nine cups all proudly exhibited. The man has his arms folded, but they are folded in the opposite way to what is natural, suggesting that his success has been achieved his way and not by the usual means.

Sometimes considered as another 'wish' card in the Tarot deck, the Nine of Cups provides confirmation that your goals are achievable and should be seen as encouraging in a reading or spread.

This card can represent pride in accomplishments, pure enjoyment, satisfaction and pleasure. It reinforces feeling good about yourself in general and having a high self-esteem.

Notes

Ten of Cups

Harmony

Family ties

Gratitude

Re-uniting

End of bad times

Forgiveness

Counting your blessings

A day out

Aided recovery

Marriage counselling

New family home

Family holiday

Welcoming

Visiting relatives

Celebrating

Feelings of joy

Feeling united

Experiencing good times

Sunshine after rain

Ten of Cups

The Ten of Cups illustrates unity and peace. In this card we see a couple embracing and joyously celebrating their achievements. They admire their house and carefully tended land before them, complete with flowing stream and mature trees. Two children dance happily beside them, and overhead are ten cups forming an arched rainbow of contentment and happiness.

This card identifies family unity and strength, also applying to a close group, team or organisation with strong bonds. It can suggest the achievement of harmony following difficulties and often the celebrations that occur with accomplishments.

The Ten of Cups can indicate being supported in times of need and also gratitude for family and close friends.

Notes

Page of Cups

Strengthening your intuition

Learning Tarot

Receiving pleasant news

Creative expansion

Innocence

Sentimentalist

Eccentricity

Being your true authentic self

Happy news

Being thoughtful

Expressing feelings of love

Learning patience

Unconditional love

Humorous

Quirky

Lighting up a room

Discovering Spirituality

Apologising

Page of Cups

In this card we see a young man dressed eccentrically and standing before flowing water. He holds a cup in his right hand while his other hand rests on his hip. A fish pops up from the cup and this page sees nothing unusual in this occurrence.

The Page of Cups illustrates the freedom of youth and the lack of responsibilities and pressures. It can suggest naivety or immaturity and sometimes a disregard for commitment.

This card may also indicate creativity and eccentricity, or someone who is finding themselves and their true passions. It generally refers to those with child-like qualities, who are quite intuitive, open minded, slow to make harsh judgements, and are considerate of others.

The Page of Cups can remind us not to take life too seriously and to appreciate the wonder of the world we live in.

Notes

Knight of Cups

Romantic

Being protective

Sensitive

Slow moving type

Acting cautiously

Ability to compromise

Introverted

Expressive

Gracious

Deliberate

Well intentioned

Amiable

Visionary

Tactful

Understated in appearance

Can exaggerate

Looks for a deeper meaning

Non-confrontational

Non-judgemental

Humanitarian

Knight of Cups

The Knight of Cups reveals a slow-moving white horse about to cross over water. Its rider is the Knight of Cups and his armour and robes all appear softer and more feminine in pattern and style. He holds his cup directly before him as though his heart will lead the way. He is on flat land but prepares himself, mentally for the mountains ahead.

This card, and whomever it personifies, may be imaginative, caring, intuitive and non-judgemental in their approach. They can be highly protective of those closest to them and also defend many humane causes.

This card may appear in a reading as heart felt or good news, offering emotional happiness and wellbeing.

Notes

Queen of Cups

Leading by example   Compassionate

               Healer   Dislikes confrontation

Psychic ability

                         Acts of kindness

Intuitive

Spiritual   Understanding

Respectful of feelings   Supports those less fortunate

Thinks deeply   Nurse

Sensitive   Has an inner knowing

Heightened senses   Patience

Natural therapist

                      Yoga instructor

           Demonstrates empathy

Queen of Cups

The Queen of Cups sits at the edge of the water on a throne decorated with cherubs. Her body looks relaxed as she sits and gazes reverently at the elaborate cup in her hands. Her cup is covered and adorned with angel wings. Her cape shares a similar pattern to that of the water flowing around her.

This Queen, as a person is compassionate, loving and good natured. She reaches the heart of the matter without drama or conflict. She leads by example and is in tune with her emotions and the feelings of others.

The Queen of Cups can also relate to psychic ability and intuition. If this card appears in a reading it often serves as a reminder to be caring, patient and tolerant of others, or it may signify someone around you who has those qualities.

Notes

King of Cups

Open-minded

Composed

Diplomatic

Accepting of all cultures

Leads without tyranny

Humanitarian

Respectful

Natural therapist

Charity worker or Philanthropist

Mediator

Good in a crisis

Accepting of all types of people

Approachable

Creates an harmonious environment

Good advice giver

Confrontation can be disorientating

Makes decisions based on the needs of all involved

King of Cups

The King of Cups sits on a throne that rises out of the water seen to be flowing freely all around him. The water symbolises taking the path of least resistance. This King has a deep respect for all living things and balances equally, aspects of both the material world and the spiritual.

He is tolerant, patient and deeply intuitive and as a leader tries to see how his actions impact those around him. He is usually very broad minded and accepting of all cultures and types of people and personalities.

If this card appears in a reading it may represent a healer, teacher, alternative therapies practitioner, humanitarian, philanthropist or anyone who has a calm and tolerant approach while also possessing great wisdom.

It can also demonstrate the need to act as this king does in a situation and adopt his attitude.

Notes

Ace of Swords

Discovering the truth

Using your mind

New ideas

Uncovering deception

Justice

Resolutions

Confessing

Winning

Gaining much needed knowledge

The need for honesty

Starting a movement

Taking responsibility

Logic

Pushing through obstacles

Mental strength

Getting answers

Light bulb moment

Using language for impact

Ace of Swords

In this card, as with all the Aces, we see a hand protruding from the clouds symbolising Divine assistance. This hand holds an upright sword, with a wreath and crown circling the top of the blade. The hand in this image grips the sword firmly emphasising the strength and power of this card.

The Ace of Swords can signify winning in its upright position and losing when reversed. I often see this card as new truths being revealed or uncovering further information.

It can represent studying or learning something new, pushing through obstacles, honesty, seeking and discovering answers and problem solving.

As with any of the aces, opportunity is available to you, but your input is required to manifest your goals.

Notes

Two of Swords

Avoiding the inevitable

Holding back

Feeling stuck

Turning a blind eye

Emotionally fragile

Procrastination

Unable to make decisions

Acting defensively

Denial

Refusing to hear

Closed mind

Stubbornness

Obstinance

Resistance

Stagnation

Opinionated

What are you missing?

Emotional blockages

Self-protection

Two of Swords

In the Two of Swords we see a woman sitting on a stone bench in front of a rocky beach front. She is blindfolded and protects herself with two crossed swords.

This card can represent an unwillingness to face the truth. It can indicate an avoidance of the facts for fear of the consequences or disruption caused.

The Two of Swords can let you know that there is something you are missing. The answer may be right in front of you, but you are failing to notice.

It may advise of the need to lower your guard and remove the barriers you have created, either as emotional protection, or through stubbornness or inflexibility. This card can also depict short sightedness.

Notes

Three of Swords

Heart issues
Heart break
Rejection   Loss
Loneliness
Grief
Extremely bad day

Emotional pain

Love triangle

Storms

Feeling at your lowest

Separation

Moving on

Letting go

Mental strain

Consequences

Growth through change

New beginnings

Indigestion

Wanting to be isolated
Extreme anxiety or panic attack
Nervous breakdown

Three of Swords

In the Three of Swords we see a red heart penetrated by three swords. There are large clouds at the top of the image and rain falls around the pierced heart.

This card can often be feared when it appears in a reading as it depicts loss, grieving, pain and heartache but there are positive aspects in its message as well.

The number three can signify new beginnings and suggest the need to see past the pain of loss and know there is better ahead. Grief is a necessary part of the healing process but grieving for too long can be unhealthy both for yourself and within relationships. The Three of Swords reminds us of this and recognises both the pain and the need to move forward.

This card may also indicate the frustration of losing a material possession, contract or anything that held significance.

It is also one of the few tarot cards that shows us weather conditions, in this case, rain.

Notes

Four of Swords

Time out

Relaxing

Honours

Accolades

Consolidating

Rest

Contemplation

Peace

Recognition

Stillness of both mind and body

Preparation

Meditation

Quieting the mind

Forced break

Recuperation

Removing distractions

Mental preparation

Re charging

Praying

Homeless

Reward or rest after accomplishment

Four of Swords

In the Four of Swords we see a man lying on a tomb, or some may see it as a bench. The room contains a stained-glass window and above the man three swords float, with a fourth sword decorating the bench below him. He lies with his hands in prayer suggesting meditation and mental stillness.

This card can signify taking a break from normal routines and activities. It represents the need to rest both mind and body in order to rejuvenate and revive energy levels.

It may depict recuperation following an illness, time out from a hectic schedule, and also mind preparation before an important event.

Notes

Five of Swords

Conflict

Dominance

Bullying

Antagonist

Imbalance of power Winning at the expense of others

Gloating

Creating enemies

Self-protection

Greed

Interrupting a crime

Security guard

Loss of integrity

Losing friendships

Interception

Selfishness

Winning in a competition

Protecting what's yours

Sweating the small stuff

Experiencing hostility

Five of Swords

In this card we see a figure with three swords in his possession and another two at his feet. He appears to have won a battle against his two opponents who walk away despondently. He wears a smug and satisfied look on his face. The sky and clouds capture the unsettled environment.

The Five of Swords represents the desire to win at all costs. It often alludes to those petty arguments that go back and forth without resolution. It can suggest winning an argument, or battle, but losing far more.

This card may indicate the need for self-defence in certain circumstances when faced with difficult people or conflicts.

It may also represent losing your moral compass or letting ego overtake empathy.

Notes

Six of Swords

Leaving something behind

Better times ahead

Moving forward slowly

Change of location

Re-location

Running away

Being rescued

Refugee

Taxi

Seeking refuge

Low level depression

Uber driver

Regaining mental health

Forced journey

The worst is over

Feeling blue

Carrying your troubles around with you

Moving out of troubled times

Moving from troubled waters to smooth

Six of Swords

In this card we see a mother and child being ferried by a man, from rough waters to smoother sailing in a small boat or raft. The woman's head is covered, and the group are surrounded at the front of the boat by six overturned swords. Ahead of them, in the far distance is land and vegetation. In this card it is not shown in its natural green state but as a blue horizon.

The Six of Swords can represent movement forward from troubling times, hence the rough waters to smooth, but there is the suggestion that this phase is not completed as yet and there may be further efforts needed to be totally clear of difficulties. It is a good sign to see though, as it can confirm that you are on the right path.

This card can indicate a period of feeling blue or down but alternatively it can also represent renewed hope following hardship.

Notes

Seven of Swords

Deception   Stealing   Dishonesty

Sneaking away   Shirking responsibilities

Getting away with something

Hiding the truth

Re-claiming something that was yours

Keeping a secret

Taking off

Stealing away for a break

Taking work home

Wanting to be alone

Stealing information

Shopping bargains   Taking more credit than is due

Playing mind games

Covering your footsteps

Seven of Swords

In this card we see a man running off with five swords in his hands while two swords remain behind him. His movements suggest he is being light footed in his effort not be caught and he looks back to check his progress.

The most common interpretation of the Seven of Swords is that of deception. It can depict a person of bad moral character, a thief and sneakiness.

It may suggest that someone will take all that they can get, and in turn, be labelled as selfish. The seven of swords can also demonstrate a lack of commitment, laziness, avoidance and lying.

When this card appears look at all possible meanings before jumping to the usual conclusion. It may be suggesting that it's time to 'steal away' for a much-needed break, or just the requirement of solitude in your life. At times we may need to be a little selfish for our own good.

Notes

Eight of Swords

Feeling trapped

Inability to see beyond current situations

Kidnapping

Jailed

Restrictions

Helplessness

Feeling like a victim

Pessimism

Self-imposed bindings

Wanting a holiday

Communication breakdown

Job dissatisfaction

Feeling defeated

Not thinking clearly

Suffering confusion

Being bound by circumstances

Staying in a fractured relationship

Eight of Swords

The Eight of Swords shows a woman loosely tied and blindfolded and surrounded by a fortress of eight overturned swords. The terrain around her is lacking in vegetation suggesting desolation and despair. She has a toe seemingly touching water symbolising that her feelings are at the forefront of her issues.

This card may indicate being trapped in a bad relationship, business, job or even stuck indoors when everyone else is out having fun.

It can represent feeling bound or stuck in circumstances that you feel are beyond your control. It suggests despair and discouragement of your current circumstances. When this card appears in a reading, it sends the message that no one is ever truly bound and there is always a solution to every problem.

Notes

Nine of Swords

Nightmares

Insomnia

Worry

Emotional despair

Overactive mind

Anxiety attack

Crying

Feelings of guilt

Desolation

Tormented

Everything seems worse at night

Being overloaded

Regret

Darkest before dawn

Beating yourself up

Sleepless nights

Low self-esteem

Grief

Wanting to turn back time

Nine of Swords

In the Nine of Swords we see a person sitting up in bed as though being woken from a nightmare, holding their hands to their face in despair and worry. The wall is lined with nine swords. The bed cover is richly symbolised and the bed itself has a violent scene engraved on its base.

This card tells of the worries and concerns that can make sleep difficult and always seem so much greater at night. It can represent an overactive mind, anxiety and panic.

When this card appears, it can let you know that you are allowing your fears to get the better of you, and in turn, may be causing yourself distress and insomnia. Dealing with any issues as they arise, or being proactive in your attitude, might be a healthier way to manage your situation.

Notes

Ten of Swords

Being gossiped about

Feeling at your lowest

Being indisposed

Being pinned down

The only way is up

Losing

Arrest

Glimmer of hope

Back-stabbing

Back surgery

Acting like a Martyr

Being caught out

Lacking strength

Negative mindset

Wallowing in self-pity

Feeling like a victim

Things can only get better

Hitting rock bottom

Darkest before dawn

Ten of Swords

In the Ten of Swords we see a man lying face down on the ground with ten swords protruding from his back. It is not the happiest looking card in the deck and its meaning is quite clear and forceful. The sky is dark and heavy but there is a glimmer of sunlight as another day dawns. This is the message of the Ten of Swords.

When you see this card appear in a reading it can warn you of gossip, backstabbing, being at your lowest or generally hitting rock bottom.

What we can take from this card as a positive, is that the expression 'It's always darkest before dawn' is often significant to remember when facing any of your own darkest times. This card is excessive in its depiction so that we get the important advice it sends.

On a lighter note, it can also point to having a bad day where nothing seems to go right.

Notes

Page of Swords

Period of study

Internship

Taking responsibility

Acting fairly

Research

Unlocking potential

Gossip

Starting a movement

Creating propaganda

New concepts

Learning as you go

Devising a plan

Developing an interest

Searching for answers

Academic ability

Creating a manual

Receiving an email, text message or letter

Seeking the truth

Page of Swords

This card shows a young person standing with their sword raised in a forward motion while they look back as though waiting for direction and approval before striking. The atmosphere depicts movement, with wind and cloud formation all flowing in the same direction as the young page would like to progress.

The Page of Swords depicts the gaining of knowledge through applying the mind, be that study, research or developing new concepts and ideas.

This page can represent all matters of fairness and also ethical issues. It can ask that you use your mind for good, to benefit yourself, and others.

The Page of Swords will suggest truth and honesty, fairness and communication. A word of warning though, this page can be a gossip, so take note of how this card presents itself in a reading to find the meaning that is appropriate for you.

Notes

Knight of Swords

Unexpected news

Intensity

Natural leader

Persistence

Haste

Speed

Comedian

Outspoken

Rude

Knowledgeable

Lacking tact

Influencer

High achiever

High intelligence

Gifted

Intense

Unemotional

Enthusiastic

Witty

Fast thinker

Speaking without thinking first

Generates excitement

Heated debate

Knight of Swords

In this card we see a knight in armour on a white horse. The knight's red cape flies behind him as he and his horse charge forward in such a hurry, with force and determination. The knight in this card charges against the wind letting nothing stand in his way.

The Knight of Swords can speak without thinking at times and yet at others, be very concise and articulate. They may be very eager to make a point and can deliver advice knowledgeably. This knight can lack sensitivity and demonstrate impatience.

The Knight of Swords may appear as a person, or sometimes represent the sudden receiving of news or information. This card can also depict reckless or spontaneous behaviour.

Notes

Queen of Swords

Straight forward

Focused and intent

Honest

Lives by the rules

Open and direct

Can be witty

Well read

Difficult to outsmart

Harsh

Likes to take control

Truthful

Gets to the point

High intellect

Public speaker

Initiates change

Teacher

Delegator

Can be humourless

Imparts knowledge

Human rights representative

Queen of Swords

The Queen of Swords sits upright on her throne and focuses her vision directly at her target. In her right hand she holds her sword in its upright position, symbolising truth and justice. Her left hand is extended out in front of her as she delivers her message with conviction. She is surrounded by clouds which can symbolise change, movement, higher thoughts and ideas. Her robe is also decorated with clouds. We also see butterflies on her crown and throne signifying greater awareness, knowledge and transformation.

This queen communicates directly and truthfully. She can be very sharp in the deliverance of her dialogue. She will speak from experience and understanding but still manage to see the humour in life and use it to soften her blow.

If the Queen of Swords appears in your reading it might represent a person with these character traits, or a situation where a direct but honest approach is required.

Notes

King of Swords

Intellectual

Extremely knowledgeable

Articulate

Story-teller

Good communicator

Professor or teacher

Researcher

Mathematician

Executive

Analytical

Uses logic over emotion

Methodical

Straightforward and direct

Politician

Non-fiction Author

Speech writer

Objective

Highly moral and ethical

Law enforcer

Highly academic

King of Swords

The King of Swords sits on a throne decorated with the symbolic butterflies. He stares directly in front of him and holds his sword in its upturned position signifying truth and justice. He is surrounded by the usual clouds associated with the swords suit, but in this card, both the clouds and the vegetation are still, reflecting the calm and balanced state of this king.

The King of Swords is very articulate and intelligent. He could be a public speaker, teacher, lawyer or any professional person in command of their language and with the acquired knowledge to match.

He is extremely logical, fair and just when managing people and will always have a high code of ethics and morals.

In a reading this card can represent any person or situation where truth, honesty and fairness are required. Communication and intelligence are also indicated by the King of Swords.

Notes

Getting to know your deck

Major Arcana

The Major Arcana consists of twenty-two of the seventy-eight cards making up a full tarot deck. These cards start with the Fool numbered zero, and go through to the World, number twenty-one.

The reason they are called the 'majors' is due to them representing the more significant occurrences in our life, the events, situations, and also people crucial to our development and progress. This is why it is important to take notice when the majors appear in your spreads or readings. They are a good indicator of meaningful or profound happenings, be that within a situation, or referring to an important person. Know that essential changes are in the air when you see a major arcana card.

One way of understanding the role of the majors is through the story of the Fool's journey. The Fool's journey was created as a means to understand, capture and demonstrate how the experiences we go through on our own journey in life, take place for a reason, and also to strengthen and prepare us for whatever lies ahead. Life is full of twists and turns, challenges and rewards. It's hard to really know happiness without first knowing pain or hardship. Everything has a beginning and an end, and the majors are there to highlight one, or many instances of importance throughout those pivotal times in our life.

The Fool's Journey

* Please note that I have used 'He' when describing the Fool in this story, but as with any of the cards in the tarot, either male or female energies may be present, or apply.

0 - The Fool: The Fool feels free and confident. He takes that first step without fear or concern for consequences, hoping that all will be well but having no real assurance of that.

1 - The Magician: The fool encounters the Magician who teaches him to use all the resources available to him to bring his ambitions and ideas to life.

2- The High Priestess: The High Priestess is the Fool's spiritual teacher. Instructing the Fool to realise the potential of his intuition, to listen, and take notice of how often we need to acknowledge what we know inwardly versus that, of which we have physical proof.

3 - The Empress: The Empress represents the Fool's mother and also mother of the earth. She is a nurturing, caring and stable influence. The Empress has great practical knowledge and experience giving her both wisdom and success.

4: The Emperor: The Emperor is the Fool's father figure and teaches him the importance of being authoritative, strong minded, practical, direct, just and fair in all his actions and interactions.

5 - The Hierophant: The Hierophant educates the Fool on the value of traditions, cultural beliefs and the importance of both learning and teaching. The Fool also discovers the ability to explore his position within a group.

6: The Lovers: The Fool is introduced to love and marriage, or the strong emotional and physical connection shared by two people, but often obstructed and confused by temptation and the need to make critical moral choices.

7 - The Chariot: The Chariot enters the Fool's life as a reminder to push through any obstacles, staying on track and striving to achieve his desires, plans and ambitions.

8 - Strength: Here the Fool is reminded of his inner strength and the power of being quietly confident and of having a firm, yet gentle approach when necessary.

9 - The Hermit: The Hermit encourages the Fool to take some well needed time out. He advises him to use this time to reflect on all that has been learned and how that knowledge can be put to good use.

10 - The Wheel of Fortune: The Wheel of Fortune appears out of nowhere as a reminder that nothing in our journey stays the same forever. Life can change unexpectedly at any given moment. This can be for the better or for the worse. Expect the unexpected.

11 - Justice: The Fool learns to take responsibility for his actions and discovers the need to pay his dues, when necessary, to find balance in life.

12 - The Hanged Man: The Fool's world, as he knows it, is turned upside down and he is urged to look at his life from a different perspective. This takes time and is beneficial to how the Fool advances.

13 - Death: The Fool is reminded at this stage that nothing stays the same forever. Often through misfortune or inconvenience, we are guided to a better outcome, even though this may not be apparent at the time. By this understanding, difficult times are easier to embrace and manage.

14 - Temperance: Temperance reminds the Fool that balance can be achieved. It is possible to have everything align and be in harmony with itself. These times are to be appreciated and valued.

15 - The Devil: The Fool knows, at this stage, that it is easy to fall into the trap of the material world. Addictions, physical wants and needs all serve to hinder the Fool's progress and he is forced to take notice of what is keeping him trapped.

16 - The Tower: The Fool discovers the feeling of his world disintegrating through sudden and unexpected events. At the time, the fear and dread are overwhelming but once the cloud of despair clears, the Fool is able to realise the potential to rebuild and move forward.

17 - The Star: The Star fills the Fool with hope. Hope is the first step towards realising your dreams and desires. Without hope there is no beginning.

18 - The Moon: The Fool sees only the shadows of the moon reflected much larger than they really are, causing him to be fearful and uneasy. He knows this is only an illusion and that he needs to slow his overactive mind and imagination.

19 - The Sun: The Fool wakes to a bright new day and a new beginning. He is inspired by the freedom he feels and is grateful for another chance and opportunity to live life to its fullest.

20 - Judgement: The Fool feels so happy and free enabling him to forgive all from the past and see it as an integral part of his development. Inner peace is felt.

21 - The World: The World completes the cycle for the Fool, and he is now ready to move forward to the next chapter of his life, well equipped and experienced enough to manage whatever transpires.

Minor Arcana

The minor arcana forms the balance of the seventy-eight tarot cards and include four suits of cards, as in playing cards, but with the inclusion of a knight. These four suits correspond to the elements of the Universe and are fire, earth, air and water. The elements are an important part of your tarot study as they give you an indication of the personality, or function of each suit. Having this knowledge gives you the ability to interpret the story, or guidance, of the cards within a spread or a reading.

- **Wands - Fire:** - Action, enthusiasm, motivation, passion (Aries, Leo, Sagittarius)

- **Pentacles - Earth:** - Materialism, money, health, physical (Taurus, Virgo, Capricorn)

- **Swords - Air:** - communication, correspondence, thoughts (Gemini, Libra, Aquarius)

- **Cups - Water:** - feelings, emotions, intuition (Cancer, Scorpio, Pisces)

The minor arcana in tarot represent the everyday thoughts, feelings, motions, communications and actions of a spread or reading. They give us insight into the steps and approaches required to answer any questions asked of the cards. Their relationship to surrounding cards, or even on their own, can give valuable information, guidance and provide a scenario that can resonate with the questioner, be that yourself or the **querent** (the person you are reading the cards for).

The minor arcana starts with an Ace, as the number one card, and goes through to the number ten. The Ace represents the commencement or beginning and as the numbers increase, so does the journey of advancement through that particular suit.

Each suit includes a set of court cards. The court cards consist of the Page, Knight, Queen and King. The court cards are usually representative of people, and their personalities vary depending on their suit. The courts can also refer to the querent themselves or can identify an aspect of the querent's attitude or character that may need adjusting.

When encountering a court card in a spread or reading, firstly take a look at the position of the card and ask yourself if it is representing a personality type, therefore it could be a person.

Alternatively, look at whether or not it is asking that the personality traits of the card drawn are required to be noted in your reading. For example, the King of swords could appear in a spread asking about your managerial work role. It may be letting you know that you need to be a lot clearer, or more assertive with your communication, bringing clarity and objectivity to the situation.

The position of a court card in a spread, be it past, present or future, is an important aspect of how the court card is read but knowing they can be both a person and personality trait will help you with your interpretation.

You can use these explanations below to help you understand the court card characters.

The Page, as a personality, usually indicates youthfulness or someone young. It can also emphasise inexperience, immaturity, innocence and a level of development. The pages are open to learning and their traits depend on the suit to which they belong.

- The Page of Wands will be daring, excitable, motivated and energetic.
- The Page of Pentacles will be practical, conscientious, efficient and sensible.
- The Page of Swords will be curious, questioning, sceptical and interested.
- The Page of Cups will be emotional, intuitive, affectionate, creative and caring.

The Knight, as a personality, usually indicates someone who acts on matters. The type of action of each Knight depends on the element of their suit.

- The Knight of Wands will act with motivation, inspiration, impulsively or enthusiastically.
- The Knight of Pentacles will act with caution, routine, consistency and without haste.
- The Knight of Swords will act with speed, volume, fearlessly and with determination.
- The Knight of Cups will act with concern, love, with feeling and empathy.

The Queen, as a personality usually indicates experience and the application of that experience depending on the element of the suit.

- The Queen of Wands will usually demonstrate attractiveness, be a motivator, be energetic or athletic, and also manage people and projects excellently.

- The Queen of Pentacles will usually demonstrate practicality, dependability, be hospitable, generous and also resourceful.

- The Queen of Swords can be very direct and unemotional in her communication. She has the ability to assess matters and people quite quickly and can often have a good sense of humour.

- The Queen of Cups is often very spiritual and intuitive, caring, kind-hearted and demonstrates patience and understanding.

The King, as a personality usually indicates the most experienced and dynamic of all the court characters.

- The King of Wands is the master of originality and can be an inspiring leader and motivator. This king can be very charming, attract attention and also be very daring and fearless when it comes to taking risks or attacking challenges.

- The King of Pentacles is usually very successful and accomplished in material matters. He can be extremely reliable and dependable in any situation and has the ability to create structure and balance.

- The King of Swords is usually intensely direct when communicating. He/ She can be quite knowledgeable and intelligent, articulate and authoritative. They enforce fairness and act with high moral standards.

- The King of Cups will be patient, kind-hearted and a good listener or therapist. They are usually very patient and tolerant, can be compassionate, loving, nurturing and affectionate. As a leader they promote and encourage a harmonious work or group environment.

A little on Numerology

When I first learned Tarot, I was given some information on how numerology can be incorporated into your understanding of the cards and their placement in a reading. I personally found this to be a very useful tool and have often referred to numerology in my own practice to bring clarity to my readings.

Feel free to explore numerology further if, like me, you find it useful and helpful in expanding your knowledge.

The following is a small example of how the numbers of the cards can have significance and add another dimension to your interpretation and translation of the reading you perform.

0: Freedom, nothing, the ultimate beginning of something, full circle

1: New beginnings, solitude, winning, leadership, the creation or potential of projects, plans or relationships, getting started, taking the first step. A seed is planted. In tarot readings the repeated appearance of the number one can be a prediction of creating something new or starting afresh.

2: Partnerships, balance, love or marriage, opposites, duality, intuition

3: Growth, creativity, friendships, early stages of success, multi-tasking

4: Stability, foundations, patience, hard work, persistence, control, being rigid or closed minded

5: Instability, conflict, impulsive or spontaneous, loss, change for both positive or negative, arguments or disagreements, courage, concern, adventure, letting go

6: Structure, harmony, family oriented, protection, care and compassion, flow

7: Gaining strength, spirituality, intuition, wishful thinking, reflection, review, evaluation

8: Strength, movement, business success, action, positive changes, power, activity, possibilities

9: Endings, completion, fulfilment, overcoming obstacles, responsibility

10: 1 + 0 = 1 …….And so we start again

For Major Arcana numbers over 9, reduce the numerals to a single digit by adding them together, for example, the World card is number 21 therefore 2 + 1 = 3

When doing a reading or a spread and you find two or more of the one number, then you could assume that the energy of that number may be more apparent or applicable to the scenario along with the traits of cards.

In this three card 'Situation, Advice and Outcome' spread, the appearance of cards all numbered five can be an indication of instability, loss and depression, but also depict courage, being supported and seeking help through an institution, or by traditional methods. The numerology reinforces the tarot card meanings.

For some readers, astrology can be an important aspect of tarot, but it is not an area I have chosen to pursue. That doesn't mean it isn't something that you may wish to investigate further at some stage. This book is focused more on you picking up your cards and starting to familiarise yourself with them, their meanings and context within a spread or draw.

Colours of the Tarot

'Rainbows are a reminder that life is not all black and white'

Colour can be an important part of learning the tarot and assisting you in getting a feeling for the energy of the cards drawn in a spread, and for a particular query.

Colour forms a part of the symbolism of the tarot and it has helped me to see at a glance what the main theme of my spread is.

The fours suits of tarot have certain dominant colours that reflect the energy of the suit. These colours are based on the elements of the suit, as mentioned previously.

Wands reflect the colours of fire: red, orange, yellow

Pentacles reflect the earthy colours of gold, brown and green

Swords reflect the light blues and light and dark greys. The Swords cards both in their meaning and their colour include a lot of light and dark shades. I consider the Swords to be the 'lesson' cards of the deck, as you may often find that when they show up in your reading, a changing of one's mindset is required.

Cups reflect the colours of emotion and feelings, red, pink and the lightest blue

The colours in the Rider Waite deck are very limited but give you the ability to get a feeling as to the influencing energy of your spread. With practice, you may be able to tell at a glance the mood of your Querent and any challenges they might be facing or alternatively, the developments of a positive nature in the Querent's life.

At some stage, after mastering the Rider Waite system and moving on to experiment with other decks, you will probably notice the way artists have used colour in the creation of their tarot cards. It is often used in exactly the same manner as in the Rider Waite deck, to provide symbolism, through colour, and to match the energy of the card's images and meanings.

Below is a chart of colours and what they can represent. I have added this chart for those who have an interest in the energy of colour.

RED: Love, Passion, Power, Desire, Strength, Courage, Anger

BROWN: Earth, Stability, Materialism, Stability, Consistency, Security

YELLOW: Happiness, Sunshine, Freedom, Success, Rejoicing, Excitement, Celebration, Creativity

ORANGE: Motivation, Ambition, Determination, Warmth, Enthusiasm, Spontaneity, Movement

GOLD: Prosperity, Winning, Material gain, Good health, Material growth, Financial security, Awareness, Enlightenment, Intensity

GREEN: Growth, Fertility, Healing, New beginnings, Peace, Harmony, Nature, Development

PURPLE: Psychic ability, Calmness, Compassion, Spirituality, Knowing, Karma

BLUE: Spirituality, Serenity, Flow, Intellect, Thought, Communication

WHITE: Purity, Innocence, Clarity, Beginnings, Lightness, Brightness, Divine intervention

GREY: Depression, Instability, Stress, Low-spirited, Shady, Uncertainty

BLACK: Fears, Worry, Darkness, Negativity, Gloom, Grief, Loss, Mystery, Misery, Dishonour, Shame, Hidden, Deceit

Here is an example of colour dominating in a spread.

In this three card spread, we can see an abundance of yellow indicating happiness, sunshine, rejoicing and celebration.

Symbols on The Cards

Each of the cards in your deck will have traditional symbols within their imagery that mean something and can add value to your reading ability.

If you are a visual learner, it is more likely that you will retain the images of the cards before you retain the key meanings. Knowing the symbols could be a useful tool triggering a recall of the meanings and messages contained in the cards.

There is no need to memorise them at first, but as you practice daily, you could use this list to help you understand what is coming through for you. Over time, you will find that eventually you won't need to constantly check but will have a good grasp of the cards drawn and what they represent. I am still not totally familiar with all the symbols and it has never hindered my reading ability, but as with anything you wish to master, knowledge and practice will always be beneficial.

Dog: Companionship, Loyalty, Guide, Guardian, Friend, Family, Love

Cat: Companionship, Spirited, Defensive, Independent, Fearless

Horse: Mode of Transport, Movement, Strength, Power, Action, Dependable

Lion: Courage, Strength, Assertiveness, Bravery

Rabbit: Fertility, Swiftness, Good natured, Softness

Snake: Rebirth, Transformation, Flow, Fluidity, Spiritual guidance, Transition, Healing

Wolf: Assertiveness, Solitude, Nocturnal activity, Darkness, Ringleader, Emotional attachment

Bird: Freedom, Protection, Advancement, New beginnings, Flight

Lizard: Regeneration, Guardian, Adaption, Intuition, Luck, Facing fears, Goal setting, Shrewdness

Butterfly: Gentleness, Mischievous, Movement, Change, Transformation, Spirit energy, Gracefulness, Knowledge, Greater awareness

Dragonfly: Maturity, Transformation, Awareness, Power, Strength, Speed, Transformation, Self-realisation

Snail: Patience, Letting go, slowing down, Determination, Strength, Perseverance, Moving forward, Progress, Balance, Knowledge

Fish: Feelings, Emotions, Fluidity, Flow, Intelligence, Endurance, Survival, Independence, Spontaneity, Abundance, Enlightenment, Good luck, Fertility, Happiness

Pentagram: The Five Elements (Spirit, Air, Earth, Water and Fire) Truth, Abundance, Harmony, Health, Protection

Infinity Figure: (Sideways Figure 8) Eternity, Continuity, Everlasting, Infinite, Spirituality, Love, Empowerment, Continuous motion, Inspiration, Balance

Angels: Protection, Guidance, Balance, Divine messengers

Cherub: Angelic innocence, Purity, Love, Closeness to God

Moon: Intuition, Mystery, Shadow, Shady, Deception, Fear, The Moon card can also represent timing in a reading, for example, around the time of a full moon.

Keys: Hidden knowledge, Security, Unlocking the pathway to knowledge (learning) Trust, Loyalty

Stars: Guidance, Good luck, Purity, Hope, Light, Change, Imagination, Inspiration, Navigation

Water: Birth, Fertility, Rejuvenation, Purity, Wisdom, Grace, Healing, Relationship, Higher consciousness

Fire: Wisdom, Knowledge, Power, Authority, Strength, Emotion, Anger, Destruction, Passion, Impulsiveness

Mountains: Spiritual elevation, Achievement, Goals, Responsibilities

Roses and Lilies: Love, Purity, Success, Manifestation of desire

Wind: Change, Motion, Challenges, Instability,

There are more symbols within the Rider Waite Tarot that are not mentioned here. You may wish to examine those further once you feel you are well into understanding your cards.

Exercises for the Visual Learner

An interesting way for a visual learner to retain any key meanings of importance to them is to draw the action or meaning on paper. It doesn't have to be elaborately done. A stick figure drawing will suffice. Firstly, write the key meaning, or your own meaning, in your own words at the top of the page. Draw an image below this that is your interpretation and description of the action.

This exercise works by allowing you to retain an image in your mind rather than a word or sentence. Once it is locked in you will retain it and be able to recall the image when needed, therefore recalling the meaning associated with the image.

It may seem like a lot of pictures to draw but as I said, they don't need to be elaborate, large or detailed. They don't need to be in colour either. As long as you know what you have drawn and it means something to you, then it will be retained as such. This can be done over time and as you feel the need. You can keep the drawings contained to a book if you prefer, or you can use scrap paper, draw the picture and then throw the paper away. Once you have drawn the picture, the image will be retained by you and there is no need to keep it recorded anywhere.

I am confident in the success of this exercise as I have used it with my Son in his struggles with Dyslexia and this method helped him to retain and recognise difficult words. By familiarising yourself with the cards in this way, you will find that eventually you will be able to pick up any Tarot deck and work with it, even playing cards (Cartomancy) if you wish.

Another way to familiarise yourself with your deck and its characters and actions is through television, movies, social situations, your workplace, school or within any other real-life interactions. Observing the characters in a movie may help you distinguish some of the traits of the suits in Tarot. It's called 'thinking in Tarot' and it really does help you understand the deck that much more. You might get a sense of the Tower card in an action movie or the Two of Cups in a romantic situation. The Lovers card may be present where there is infidelity in a marriage, or workplace disagreements could remind you of the Five of Wands. The possibilities are endless because, after all, Tarot is our tool offering guidance in all areas of our lives and with every conceivable situation.

Shuffling your Cards

Shuffling is one thing that all Tarot readers need to know how to do. Having a well shuffled deck will help ensure a good and accurate draw of the cards.

For those who have never played cards, shuffling may be tricky to grasp, but eventually you will find a method that suits you.

I have never been great at shuffling cards and shuffle from the back to the front of the deck with my right hand while I hold the cards in my left hand. (I'm right-handed) Some readers like riffle shuffling which is often seen at casinos or when using playing cards. It is sometimes not as easy to do with tarot cards as they have more cards in a deck and the thickness can vary. Riffle shuffling can bend your cards over time, and this can be another negative aspect of that type of shuffling.

Another way to shuffle your cards thoroughly is to spread them all out over a table or desk face down and swirl them around a few times until you feel they have been mixed around enough. You then gather them up and draw your cards for a spread or reading. This is usually called 'finger painting' because the motion is similar. This method can only really be used if you work with reversals (Upside down cards), which I will cover a bit later in the book.

For those who don't like to hold their cards and hand shuffle, or have hand injuries or arthritis, an alternative way is to place your deck on the table and cut it into three plies. You can then keep cutting your piles until you feel the cards have been mixed through enough. This can be quite time consuming but is still a viable method.

Whichever method you choose, make sure you are thorough. Getting the same cards come up in a draw as the one before is not always a coincidence and may just come down to bad shuffling. If you have shuffled extremely well and the same cards come through again, then I would see that as a loud and clear message from the cards, and in turn, the Universe.

After shuffling the cards thoroughly, my practice is to cut the cards into three piles. I take the top card, or cards, from the middle deck to use in my reading. I then place the remaining cards to the left of that pile on top of the remaining cards on the right pile. I always take a look at the card on the very bottom of my remaining stack of cards as it usually bears some significance to the question asked. You would be surprised by what information you can get by looking at that bottom card.

Sometimes cards can fall out of the deck as you are shuffling. If this happens in an unusual way, take a mental note, or write down the name of the card that fell out. Place it back into your deck and keep shuffling. It may have some significance as the reading progresses.

Drawing Cards for a Reading

While you are shuffling your deck is the important time to focus on your query or question. Asking a question either in your mind, or out loud is the best way to ensure that you get the answer, or guidance needed from the cards. Stop shuffling when you get that 'feeling' to stop. How do you know when that time is? This is unexplainable. You just do. If the cards drawn have no bearing on your question at all, then you may want to start again. It could be that you were not focused on the question or were distracted while shuffling.

You may want to write your question, or questions down in a booklet, journal or on a piece of paper. The reason I suggest this is because quite often you can forget the structure of the question asked and that can cloud your interpretation. Keep in mind that the tarot will give guidance specific to your query, so be specific in your questioning. It may be better to ask multiple questions with a draw for each one based on the information received from the previous reading. For example, If I ask the cards "How will I handle my noisy and abusive neighbours?" and the cards give me guidance suggesting that I move house, I can then do another spread, or draw asking "What would the outcome be if I should sell my house?" This could be followed up with a draw of cards asking, "If I re-locate, how will I meet, and make new friends?"

It's these kinds of specific questions that will produce the best results both for yourself and when reading for others. Even if you are only drawing one card, I really believe it to be important to have a reason for your draw, be it guidance for the day, or to find the answer to a specific query.

As a beginner, it is probably best to draw a card each day. Rather than draw that card in the morning, try drawing it at the end of the day. Take note from the key meanings I have provided in this book to see if any of them relate to the day you have experienced. As you shuffle the cards, you may want to mentally ask the question "How has my day been?" or "What has been significant in my day today?"

Alternatively, you can draw a card in the morning asking for guidance for the day. I always include the date to be extra specific in my question. Again, you can look at the key meanings of the card drawn and try to work through whatever the card is guiding you towards, or against. Try not to be fearful if a card with what looks like a negative aspect presents itself. I once drew the Ten of Swords as my daily card and was horrified at what to expect for my day ahead. As it turned out, my husband put an action movie on that night which was full of fighting, murders and knives! The Ten of Swords was spot on! Fortunately, the only ill effects I had from drawing that card were that it kept me awake because I'm an Empath (empathetic person) and I find it hard to watch violence and fighting, even if it is only a movie.

I will also add that even negative looking cards can have a positive aspect to them but may require a challenge, or change of attitude, to realise the potential advantage of their appearance.

As you practice with your cards and become more familiar with the key meanings, you can then also look at the cards you draw in a spread and take notice if any of your own additional, or alternative message comes through. This is known as using our own intuition or feeling for interpreting what presents itself. Let's face it. The cards themselves in the Rider Waite deck are quite limiting in their art and illustration. They are rich in symbolism and somebody else's creative processes, but we use them as they are, and expand our perception by bringing them, and their significance, across to our era and current circumstances.

How many men or naked babies on horseback (The Sun) do you see day to day, someone hanging upside down from a tree (The Hanged Man), or a guy dressed in tights and a dress stealing a bunch of swords (Seven of Swords). None of the Rider Waite cards have images of modern-day events or people, but they do represent character traits, actions and consequences covering any era and that is why it is so important to have a good understanding of what each card can offer in a reading today.

I recently did a reading for someone who was concerned about partnering up with someone in a business venture. This person had the potential to bring more business in through their own contacts, but they would be using all the facilities provided by my client. I drew the Six of Pentacles within the chosen spread and I instantly saw this as guidance for the querent to be sure to make any concerns clear from the outset. I saw the possibility of my client becoming a charity and only breaking even in this deal, rather than attracting the desired gain, for the good of the business. My client took this advice and weighed it all up, having several more meetings and discussions before any contracts were signed.

Tarot is an age-old system carried through many, many years of it being adapted to the current environment of each and every reader, past and present. I agree that we can't get stuck on key meanings, but I also believe them to be a necessary part of every beginner's journey into learning, and aligning, the traditional meanings with our lives today.

Spreads

Spreads are used in Tarot readings to paint a picture, tell a story, provide a plan and often to reinforce or confirm our thoughts or actions. We can gain valuable guidance through the cards on many different topics, issues and queries.

Simple spreads can be just as beneficial as lengthy ones and can be used quite often when you have a list of questions following on from each other as I have suggested earlier.

Drawing one card can offer a lot of advice on its own and can also be used in many instances. One card can be drawn for daily guidance, as a quick answer to a pressing question, to discover the underlying theme of a week, month or even year, and for many other concerns or issues. The one constant requirement is to be clear in your request from that one card draw, as with any time you shuffle, and draw cards with the aim of getting answers related to your question.

One of my favourite spreads is a three-card spread called **Situation, Advice and Outcome**.

Card 1: Situation: This card lets you know of the situation you are querying. It should be recognisable to you as the issue at hand.

Card 2: Advice: This card represents what you are advised to do in this situation for the best outcome.

Card 3: Outcome: This card lets you know what the outcome will be if you take the advice of the cards.

Another three-card spread that is very popular with beginners is the **Past, Present and Future** spread.

Card 1: Past: This card describes past events, people or actions significant to you or your querent.

Card 2: Present: This card lets you know of the current aspects of your life or that of your querent.

Card 3: Future: This card gives a possible outcome for the future based on yours, or the querent's current environment or circumstances.

The **Celtic Cross** spread is a widely used spread in tarot readings. I would consider it a necessity to learn this spread and also to practice with it often. It is a great spread for determining a timeline for events, as it can be difficult to gauge timing in tarot. The Celtic Cross spread provides us with a past, present, near future and outcome, allowing us to verify the past, to assess its impact on our near future and to determine, or confirm our actions. Although this would not be considered the first spread you try, it will probably be one of your most used, once you are familiar with your cards and their meanings and interactions with each other. The more you practice with this spread the better, even if it is confusing at first, persist.

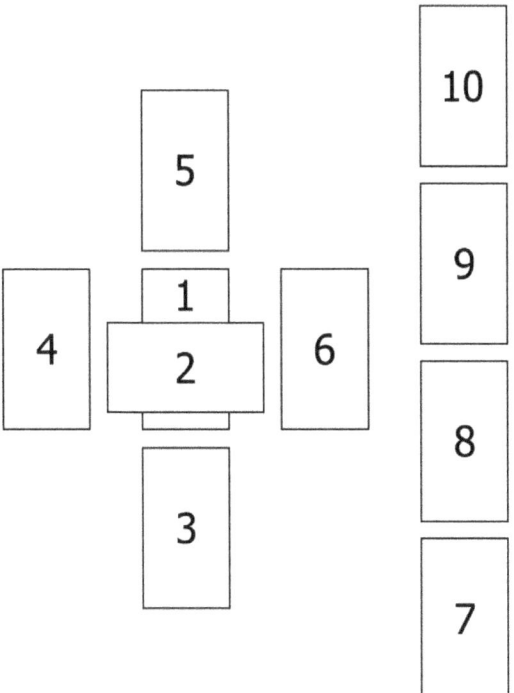

Card 1: The querent: The person involved in the reading or query.

Card 2: Crossing Card 1: This card represents what is either holding the querent back or working in their favour. These are the two main cards at this stage that will verify whether or not you have shuffled well and drawn your cards at the appropriate time. If these cards resonate with you, the querent and the situation in question, you can then continue laying further cards. If not reshuffle and focus on your question again.

Card 3: This is the situation card. It identifies the matter at hand and establishes a framework for the reading according to the question asked.

Card 4: The recent past is indicated by this card. Usually, the energy of this card is on its way out but can often play a part in the actions or guidance moving forward. In my opinion, this is another card that helps confirm the correct draw has taken place because we can usually easily identify the past.

Card 5: I have always known this card to be 'What hangs over me' or what the outcome could be. This card can often be compared to the outcome card in position 10, as it can refer to what the querent would like to happen.

Card 6: The near future. What is likely to happen next.

Card 7: What the querent brings to the situation. What is their energy like? This could have either a positive or a negative connotation and could be an indicator that the querent has the right attitude, or that their attitude and approach may need to change in order to achieve or avoid the outcome.

Card 8: This card is seen as the current environment card. It can let you know what or who may be involved in the situation. It can be known as what, or who, is hidden from the querent and could be an influencing factor.

Card 9: This card is considered to be hopes and/or fears. Sometimes they are one and the same. I like to think that if a positive card is presented here then the querent is on the right track in the way they are handling their situation. If a more negative card appears, there may be lessons or adjustments to make with either behaviour, actions or thought patterns.

Card 10: This is the outcome card based on the cards drawn for the querent and their issue or situation.
Additional spreads such as the three-card spread mentioned earlier can be drawn if advice is needed around the outcome, especially if it's not the desired outcome of the querent.

* It is important to keep in mind that we all have free will, therefore the outcome of a spread, or reading can alter if the advice of the cards is avoided or disregarded.

I will often draw extra cards once I have my Celtic Cross spread laid out if extra information is required on a particular card. I call them my expansion and clarification cards. If, for example, the near future card, number six was ambiguous to me, I would shuffle the remaining cards in my deck and as I am shuffling, I would ask the cards for expansion and clarification on card number six. I then cut my deck as per my usual method, described earlier, which is cutting into three piles and taking the top two cards from the middle deck. I would lay these two cards somewhere near to card number six and see what further information I can gather.

With any of the spreads you do, even if it is one card, you can always draw extra cards to help you expand and clarify your original draw.

There are so many good spreads available that you will come across in your research. Practice with as many as you can and find the spreads that suit you and your style of reading. Most good Tarot readers will use very few of the many accessible spreads around and will often be comfortable using three to five card spreads or the Celtic Cross.

A great book on the subjects of spreads is 'Tarot Spreads' by Barbara Moore. Barbara offers a lot of great advice, techniques and many different spreads to learn and practice with.

You can develop your own spreads quite easily. All you need to ensure is that you have your card positions defined and a question for your spread. Try creating a few of your own and see how you go. It can be a very constructive part of your practice and training. Every time you get your cards out and familiarise yourself with them, and with different spreads, the quicker it will become second nature.

Frequently Asked Questions - FAQ's

I have composed a list of frequently asked questions posed by beginners everywhere, and from all walks of life.

Rather than have chapters dedicated to these individual topics, I feel that questions and answers are somehow easier to browse through and also more easily absorbed.

I have answered to the best of my ability and with whatever works for me, but I encourage you to join Tarot groups, be they online, within social media, or in person if you live somewhere that offers you that option, and if you have the time to commit and get involved.

Beginners to Tarot can sometimes feel quite guilty about practicing. I have been told that historically it was considered a forbidden activity and it was only the very strong willed that rebelled and persisted risking their safety for the sake of their craft. I ask that if you are passionate about Tarot and about helping people, that you too persist and discover all that reading Tarot can offer, both for yourself and in the lives of those who cross your paths.

If you are new to Tarot it can be quite daunting, and let's face it, in life, asking questions is a very common way to feel connected to others and to gain knowledge from real people. I encourage you to ask, ask, ask, sort through the answers you are given, and then do it your way. There is no wrong or right way with many of the aspects of Tarot but using a common-sense approach and by trusting your intuition, you can move forward and progress, as many of us have, in providing an honest and legitimate service.

Q - What is the best deck for a beginner to buy?

A - Any of the Rider Waite Smith decks are the best decks to start you on your Tarot learning journey. They will provide you with the essential elements, symbolism and the use of colour and numerology that will be used as a foundation for you to gain a clear understanding of the Tarot. Many modern artists and deck creators have based their works on the Rider Waite system, but their use of colour and symbolism may vary, or be of a more personal and artistic nature. These decks are often very beautiful, humorous, quirky and sometimes theme based, therefore it may be more difficult, as a beginner using one of these decks, to learn the fundamental components of Tarot. Beginning your Tarot journey with the Rider Waite deck will allow you to master all the necessary fundamental elements and themes of the Tarot so that in time, you can buy many other beautiful decks that you resonate with, and enjoy discovering and performing readings using the symbolism developed by some very clever individuals.

Q - Is it true that my first tarot deck should be gifted to me?

A - This is not true at all, in my opinion. This is a superstition and has been disproved by many talented professional tarot readers all over the world.

Q - How should I store my cards?

A - You can store your cards in any way that suits you. I would recommend putting the original box they came in aside for safe keeping. It is always wise to keep the box as new as possible to retain its value should you ever want to sell it on. Having said that, as far as my research goes, not too many people sell their first study deck but if you continue to buy alternative decks, this may be relevant.
I store my individual decks in small zip bags similar to make up bags. I like to access them easily and find a zip to be more practical than a drawstring bag. They are usually lined too, which helps to keep my cards safe. I might add a couple of my favourite crystals in with whichever deck I am drawn to using at the time, just for some extra energy, cleansing and protection. That is not necessary, just a personal preference.
There are many beautiful drawstring bags available to purchase and I often store my excess decks in those and place them in a cupboard or draw alongside my packets of incense. My decks always smell lovely that way. Again, these are all suggestions so you should do whatever is comfortable for you.

Q - Are there any rituals to protect myself that I should know of, before I use my tarot cards?

A - This is a very personal preference as some people just pick up their cards and practice with no rituals or routines. Others will have quite extensive methods of preparing themselves, their reading space and their cards.
My practice is to ask my Angels, Archangels, Spirit Guides and the Divine, to surround and protect me with Divine white light, allowing only that which is for my higher and greater good, and sent with love to enter into my space. I thank my Tarot cards for allowing me to use them as a tool too which is another personal approach. I will also light some Sage incense and I often hold my deck above the incense to cleanse it of any previous readings or energy. This is also something I do with every new deck I purchase before I use it. Another method of clearing your deck between

readings is knocking on the deck three times, waving your hand across the deck and mentally saying "I clear this deck of any previous energy." You can then continue shuffling for your next reading.

Some people will suggest that you place your deck somewhere close to you when you sleep. Again, this is a personal preference. I wasn't a believer in this practice until I was familiarising myself with a particular deck that just wasn't resonating with me while I was in bed, and before I went to sleep. I packed it up and put it beside me on my bed instead of getting up and putting it away. The next day when I had another go at using the deck, it finally made sense and we worked well together, therefore, I can't dismiss this method as being madness.

When finishing a reading I will thank my Angels, Archangels, Spirit Guides and the Divine for their assistance and also, again, thank my cards.

Do what feels right for you. Using Tarot cards, in my opinion, doesn't pose too much of a problem with dark or negative energy entering your space, as compared with other practices such as house or business cleansing, or mediumship practices, where spirit energies may be more apparent, and can result in some discomfort and ill feeling. I have experienced this and can say that care must be taken in these situations.

Q - Do I need to cleanse my tarot cards at any time?

A - Many tarot readers will cleanse their decks from time to time clearing them of any energy that might be picked up during readings and with constant use.

There are a few ways to clear your deck. I use sage smudge sticks or sage incense which can be easily bought online or from a new age store and can also be used to cleanse your house or workspace of any stale or negative energy.

My personal routine before I sit down to use my cards, is to light some sage incense and place it nearby. I will run my deck through the smoke from the burning incense and ask my Angels and Spirit guides to cleanse my cards in preparation for my reading.

Another method of clearing your deck is to place all your cards back in order from major arcana through each suit until they are in order once again. You can then shuffle and commence reading.

Your deck can also be placed out under the light of a full moon to cleanse it and re-energise it but be careful of the weather conditions and make sure your deck is kept from getting damp.

Placing crystals on your deck or placing your deck near a salt lamp are other ways of cleansing, as is using Reiki if you are familiar with that practice.

Q - Is there a standard of ethics to follow when doing readings with tarot cards?

A - I believe there is, and it's a common-sense approach that really needs to be taken when you knowingly have the ability to look into the lives of others.

I will never read cards without the approval, or permission, of the person I am reading for, or more importantly, about. If somebody was to come to me and ask me to read about another person besides themselves, I will only do so based on how this person or relationship affects my client.

I will also refuse to answer questions about affairs or infidelity within relationships, but rather, I will advise my client on any areas of their own life, or behavioural patterns, that may require changing if advised by the cards. I must add here that unless you have further educational qualifications as a counsellor, lawyer, financial adviser or therapist, it would be best to refer any clients on to a professional should they have issues or problems that go beyond the guidance of a tarot reading.

Please note, that as a beginner, you may wish to practice with public identities or news and current affairs. Anything in the public domain can be used as a practice tool to test yourself and develop your understanding of the tarot.

I act without judgement when reading for others. It is not my place to have an opinion about how others choose to live their lives. My responsibility is to deliver the information and guidance as sent through the tarot cards and to answer any questions relating to those cards and the guidance they offer to my client.

Confidentiality is another important area of practicing ethically. I feel that it is important that your client, or anyone you read for, feels safe knowing that whatever is transposed in a reading will remain private and confidential. Many people open up to tarot readers and divulge information they wouldn't normally reveal, therefore trust plays a big part in the role of a good reader.

Delivering the guidance of the cards is best done in a positive way, leaving your client feeling hopeful no matter what the circumstances or nature of the reading, there are always actions that can be taken, or questions asked of the cards for every situation. It will be your duty, in my opinion, to look for the best way forward for your client.

Q - Should I keep a tarot journal?

A - As you begin practicing with your tarot cards, creating a journal of your interpretations can be a great way to record your progress. Seasoned tarot readers will often keep a journal of their personal readings and reflections, with dates and information that can be referred back to if needed, for accuracy and as a retrospective view of events and circumstances. **We all have free will and our path or journey as predicted by the cards can alter at any time**.

This is something I stress whenever I read for someone as nothing is set in stone. We may stay in an unhealthy relationship, change jobs, cancel a holiday, continue with an addiction, or any other of the endless scenarios that can alter the outcome of a reading based on what has been suggested by the cards.

Keeping a journal, especially when practicing on yourself or public situations, can be invaluable in identifying where, or where not, the advice of the cards was followed.

I have tarot journals everywhere around my house. I have many from my studying days, where I would scrapbook, or write down as many meanings as I could discover through my practice. I have journals created for different family members and others dedicated to a particular business practice that I read for. I also keep a small notepad and pen in the case holding my regularly used deck so that I can jot things down as they come up in a reading.

Q - Can I do a reading for myself?

A - This seems like an obvious 'yes' and for me it is. I enjoy reading for myself and will often check how I will go with an important occasion, problem or scenario that I need advice on. I can usually tell at a glance if it is a favourable situation, or if action will be required on my part. This didn't happen overnight, but with dedicated practice over time, and with the confidence that comes from knowing the key meanings of the cards. Colour and numerology as I explained earlier, all help to appreciate and capture the essence of the messages and themes emerging through your chosen spread.

To read for yourself you may need to consider the reading as if it were for someone else. What honest advice would you give with the client in this reading? Where do you see positivity? Where do you see elements requiring a change of attitude or mindset? Where do you observe repeated patterns, themes or numbers relating to the overall energy of the spread or reading?

I have gained enormous relief when reading my own cards during difficult times, so I highly recommend becoming accustomed to this practice.

My last piece of advice when reading for yourself, is to do so while calm and level-headed. Stress and emotion are both energies that can have an effect on drawing the appropriate cards and in your ability to interpret those cards accurately.

Q - Can I ask yes and no questions with the tarot cards?

A - When beginning tarot, it is tempting to want to experiment with yes and no questions and answers.

If, for example, I was to have answered the questions in this book with only a yes or no, I wouldn't be doing justice to the questions posed and as a result, you as the reader, would be limited in what you would gain from your learning experience.

It is no different with reading tarot. There is so much more information to be gained by the way you phrase your questions, allowing the cards to open up to you, just as if you were having a conversation, and give you as much information as they can.

A better form of questioning is to begin by asking how, what if, who, where or how, in relation to your query. This will broaden the information received, and more likely than not, result in giving you, and your client, a more informed answer.

Sometimes we do want a simple yes, or no answer and I have found that this can be achieved by choosing two cards from your deck. One for yes and the other to represent a no. Shuffle those two cards while mentally asking your question. The card you turn up when you are ready to do so will give you the yes or no answer you demanded. Keep in mind that this method is purely used to ascertain the yes or no answer you asked for but will give no other information.

I personally don't ask yes and no questions of my cards anymore. There are no guarantees with the results, and this can be detrimental to the reputation of the reader. I look at the energy of the cards drawn when posing my query and can usually gauge the outcome in other ways.

Q - Do I need to be psychic to read tarot?

A - No, you don't need to be psychic to read tarot cards, but you may find yourself becoming more open to all things of a mystical and metaphysical nature throughout your learning experience.
Expanding the use of your intuition while learning to read spreads, can open you to the power of the mind and the possibilities of having flow and synchronicity occur around you more often.
I will explain a little more on intuition. Intuition is our inner sensing without any physical knowing. It is our inner navigation system. To develop your intuition, you need to begin trusting it, and that is where a lot of us go wrong.
Everyone can relate to those times when we should have gone left, but we turned right, when we thought of someone and not long after we hear from them. Our intuition is there for a reason. Disregard it and life can be challenging. Take notice of your intuition, start acting on it, and life can seem so much easier.
Tarot readers learn to rely on their intuition and use it within their practice. I can recall many occasions early on, where I've read for someone and been hesitant to tell them of certain visions, or messages, I felt the need to pass on. Nonetheless, I did, and the response has always verified what my intuition pushed so hard for me to pass on.
You may, in your tarot journey, have no choice but to notice your developing intuition. I urge you to work on it, and with it, not only with tarot but within your life in general. Strengthening your intuition will enhance the flow of your life, your relationships and of course, your ability to read tarot significantly better.

Q - Can I make money from tarot reading?

A - Yes, you can make money from tarot reading although it can take time to be proficient enough to do a full reading and be confident in your ability.
Getting to know each card and their different aspects and applications within a spread and doing practice readings, be they on willing family and friends, on public identities or even on yourself, will be of great help in assisting you to become a competent tarot reader.
I can't stress enough the importance of taking your cards out every day, or at any opportunity, and familiarising yourself with them. The only way you will really get to know them is to use them.
Do some practice readings utilising the key meanings offered in this book and look at how the cards fit together. Notice if they have a relationship. Are the characters facing each other or is one turning its back on the other? Is there an excess of major arcana cards within your spread letting you know that more profound occurrences are imminent?
Trust your intuition to add to the key meanings provided and take notice of your first reaction when looking for answers in the cards. Trust that initial reaction, and

any other thoughts or feelings you experience throughout your reading.
You may notice over time, especially if you keep a record of your practice readings, that you will no longer need to refer to a book as often, or at all, and be happy with the outcome of your readings.

Q - What are tarot reversals, and do I need to use them?

A - Tarot reversals are cards that appear upside down in your spreads when you cut and shuffle your deck in such a way as to allow some cards to become reversed.

Upright   **Reversed**

It is probably best for beginners to focus on learning the cards in an upright manner before using reversals in their spreads and readings.
Many advanced tarot readers make a conscious choice to avoid using reversals and others believe reversed cards enhance and give more detailed information to a reading. It is a personal and individual decision to make. For every reversed card, there will be an upright card offering similar information therefore a reading can be equally as effective and detailed using only upright cards.
I suggest that you get to know your upright meanings and do your spreads and readings with only upright cards to begin with. Once you feel comfortable with your reading ability, try shuffling to create reversals and see how it feels to interpret a spread this way. You may find it comfortable and more informative, enhancing your understanding and explanation of the reading, or you might find it more difficult or confusing. There is no right or wrong decision regarding this, only personal choice. I will use reversals with some decks, including the Rider Waite, but not with others. I just do what I feel is appropriate at the time. Some modern decks don't allow for reversals with the backs of the cards having a definite top and bottom.
Shuffling the cards for reversals is quite simple. You can use the method described earlier called 'finger painting' where all seventy-eight cards are laid out face down on a table and mixed around until you feel they are shuffled thoroughly. Once you collect them and place them back into a pile, there will be reversals within your deck. Continue shuffling as normal while mentally forming the question you wish to be answered. Another way of getting reversal into your deck is to cut your deck into three piles, reverse one pile, shuffle the deck and repeat the process, shuffling again

after this and forming your question at the same time.

If you choose to use reversals in your readings, then understanding why they have appeared that way is very important when interpreting your spread. They will be based on the standard upright meaning of the card, yet the reason they are reversed will be something you will need to determine in the context of the reading.

Generally, a reversal can represent a delay, and if you feel that this is the case, it is a reminder that your issue may develop, as in its upright position, but not just yet. Patience may be required, or alternatively, further action may be needed to achieve the card's upright meaning and intention.

A reversed card can sometimes mean the opposite to that of the upright meaning, for example, the Two of Wands in its upright position, when meaning planning and laying foundations, could indicate a lack of planning and organisation when reversed.

It is important while interpreting reversals that care is taken to examine the card, or cards, surrounding the reversal and keep within the context of the reading. This can take some time and practice to get right but is only through using reversals and taking note of anything gained in your readings, that you may be motivated to continue using them.

I have added images and possible key meanings of reversals in this book for your reference and I urge you to add your own to the list. Look carefully at the reversed image in a spread and take notice of whatever jumps out at you. Your first thoughts when you consider its position, the general theme of the reading and also how you feel when you see the card are important. Again, I stress that you be guided by your intuition. While practicing as a beginner, it can be helpful to take a few minutes for a break when doing your interpretation of a spread or reading. A little time away from the pressure of trying to understand your spread can open your mind to anything you might have missed at first glance.

Reversals

The Fool Reversed

Naivety   Stupidity

Unlucky   Lack of direction

Poor judgement

Limitations   Missed opportunities

Immaturity   Held back

Hesitance

The need to let your hair down

Stagnating

Playing it safe   Dangerous behaviour

Going backwards   Delay in being free

The Magician Reversed

Deceit Manipulation

Lacking ability Laziness Lack of motivation

Greed

Meddling

Playing tricks Con artist

Untrustworthy Failure

Setbacks

Untapped talent

Writers block

Imbalance Bad timing

Delay in a project or plan Blocked

Corrupted

The High Priestess Reversed

Secretive

Inner turmoil

Ignoring intuition

Hidden truth

Bad Karma

Being kept in the dark

Untrustworthy relationships

Suppressed emotions

Unexpressed feelings

Psychic attack

Being caught off guard

Ungrounded

Materialism

The need to slow down

Dark side

Lack of empathy

The Empress Reversed

Miscarriage

Lack of guidance

Neglect

Abandonment

Heartless actions

Overdue

The need to get outdoors

Lack of nutrition

Unsupported

Wanting to go home

Miss-kept

Downturn in business

Scarcity

Lacking emotional support

Delay in achieving goals

The Emperor Reversed

Instability   Recklessness

Lack of control   Abuse

Inflexible   Untrustworthy

Avoidance   Lack of authority

Lack of structure   Lack of self-control

Untapped potential   Dispassionate

The need for direction   Lacking boundaries

The Hierophant Reversed

Breaking with tradition

Misunderstanding

Racism

Lack of routine

Bullying

Wanderlust

Manipulation

Tyranny

Breaking rules

Misunderstanding

Atheist

Breaking free

Lucking structure   Feelings of guilt

The Lovers Reversed

Relationship breakdown

Fear of commitment

Lack of spark

Affairs

Infidelity

Loss of physical attraction

Conflict within relationships

Lack of morals

Difficult choices

Divorce

Indecision

Gender confusion

Poor decision making

Lack of emotional connection

The Chariot Reversed

Inaction

Unmotivated

Lacking direction

Fear of losing

Complacency

Stagnation

Lack of preparation

Snail's pace

Car issues

Car accident

Roadblock

Being late

Undisciplined

Setbacks

Unfinished business

Rough road

Strength Reversed

Lack of control   Lack of stamina

Abuse of authority   Being unreliable

Requiring strength   Bad influence

Misused power

Lack of empathy

Untrained pet

Over controlling

Neglect

Unempowered

Abuse

Harsh words or actions

Unkindness

Coming on too strong   Loosened

The Hermit Reversed

Lack of insight   loneliness

Insecurity

Misdirected

Immaturity

Hectic schedule

Need to see a counsellor

Having no idea

Being in the dark

Lack of guidance

Unresolved

Misconception

Stress

The need to trust your intuition

Not knowing which way to turn

Wheel of Fortune Reversed

At a standstill

Stagnation

Ill fortune

Delays

Resistance

Playing it safe

Inactivity

Boredom

Sleeping in

Resisting change

Missing opportunities

Lack of faith

Narrowmindedness

Making the wrong choices

Letting obstacles stand in your way

Justice Reversed

Delay in an outcome

Cheating

Misjustice

Being unaccountable

Detention

Denying involvement

Imbalance

Shirking responsibility

Lying

Not doing your fair share

Not realising consequences

Losing a lawsuit

Acting unethically

Getting in trouble with the law

Adjournment

The Hanged Man Reversed

Holding on

Struggling

Creating blockages

Narrowmindedness

Moving too quickly

Acting in haste

Over thinking

Being selfish

Being controlling

Not seeing others point of view

Resistance

Putting yourself first

Inability to let go of something or someone

Death Reversed

Resisting the inevitable

Not admitting something is over

Realising that it's only a matter of time

Hoarding

Maintaining old ways

Co-dependency

Being stubborn

Refusing to move with the times

Maintaining an addiction

Going against the grain

Inability to let go

Beginning

Enabling bad habits

Temperance Reversed

Imbalance

Mental breakdown

Being extreme

Being excessive

Ill health

Experiencing lethargy

Striving for balance

Delayed recovery

Being scattered

Unaccepted apology

Waning

Misconception

Disconnection

Lack of flow

Anxiety

Disorientation

Disharmony

The Devil Reversed

Release

Overcoming addiction

Saying 'No'

Letting go

Discovering spirituality

Leaving a party early

Being the designated driver

Making a fresh start

Overcoming depression

Attending a support meeting

Avoiding temptation

Not getting caught up by appearances

Exposing someone of undesirable character

The Tower Reversed

Avoiding a catastrophe

Saving the day

Emergency work

Planning ahead

Luck is on your side

Finding the truth before it's too late

Avoiding embarrassment

Preparing for a storm

Avoiding exposure

Near miss

Receiving a fine over conviction

Holding on

Being given a warning

'Right place, right time'

The Star Reversed

Lack of hope

The need to be positive

Pessimism

Selfishness

Giving up

Lack of creativity

Meanness

Anxiety

Lack of spirituality

Disharmony

Suffering depression

Holding back

Not knowing

Feeling depleted

The need to have faith

The Moon Reversed

Overcoming fear

Exposing deception

Trusting yourself

Recognising anxiety

Mental clarity

Seeing your way clear

Don't let the dogs out

Being focused

Being courageous

Seeing through something or someone

Tomorrow is a new day

Between full moons

Waiting until morning to make a decision

Sabotage

The Sun Reversed

Feeling trapped

Temporary unhappiness

Lack of understanding

Lack of freedom

Bursting someone's bubble

Imposing constraints

Lacking energy

Feeling unmotivated

Staying indoors

Doing what is expected

Being unforgiving

Missing out

Lacking confidence

Feeling left out

Feeling unwell

Judgement Reversed

Lack of hope

Confusion

Feeling disillusioned

Feeling righteous

Going through therapy

Not knowing what to do

Being misjudged

Lacking purpose

Searching for answers

Stagnating

Feeling lost

Looking for recognition

Needing assurance

Feeling hard done by

Lacking direction

The World Reversed

Lack of closure

Incomplete

Travel plans cancelled

Opposing forces

Lack of care

Ignorance of world events

Wasted talent

Suffering

Hiding away from the world

Discontent

Ingratitude

Inactivity

Feeling unfulfilled

Ignorance

The feeling that something is missing

Ace of Wands Reversed

Missed opportunity

Lacking in drive

Unmotivated   Shyness   Lacking confidence

Lacks ambition

Lack of enthusiasm

Sitting on the fence

Fear of failure

Resisting the challenge

Slacking off

Stunted growth

Low self-esteem

Unimaginative

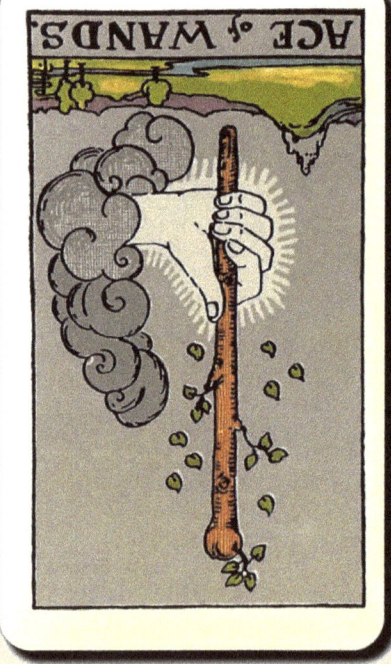

It's yours if you want to work for it

The need to rise to the challenge

Two of Wands Reversed

Disrespected

Lack of planning

Unoriginal

Cancellations

Conforming

Uninventive

Unable to lead effectively

Lack of direction

Lack of authority

Wasting time

Throwing it all away

No plans

Leaving it to fate

Uninventive

Unwilling to take a risk

Taking a back seat

Three of Wands Reversed

Unadventurous

Short-sightedness

Resisting change

Lack of planning

Lack of leadership

Setting a bad example

Taking a back seat

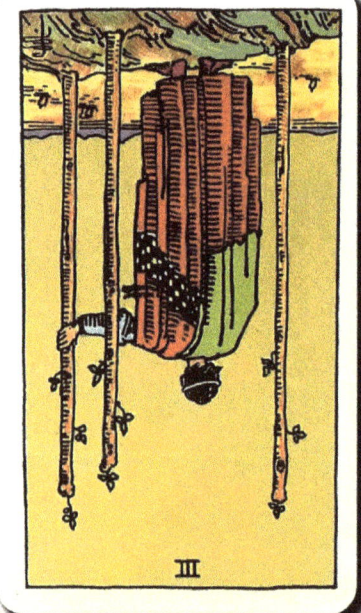

Disorganisation

Lack of foresight

Delay in getting the job done

Unable to visualise

Playing it safe

Narrowmindedness

Underdeveloped

Four of Wands Reversed

Cancelled plans

Broken Engagement

Disappointment

Missed celebration

Being conservative

Feeling stifled

Postponements

Lacking enthusiasm

Unhappy environment

Recluse

Gate crasher

Long Engagement

Not getting an invitation

Five of Wands Reversed

Avoiding arguments

Disliking confrontation

No competition

Unchallenged

Compromise

Breaking up a fight

Forgiveness

Fighting back

Calling a truce

Not letting anyone get to you

Having good manners

Teamwork

Bad sportsmanship

Demonstrating indifference

Six of Wands Reversed

Shame

Lacking acknowledgement

Disorder

Modesty

Runner up

Being humble

Missing out

Unrewarded

Low self-esteem

Not meeting criteria

Being demoted

Fear of failure

Not doing enough

Delay in reaching a target

Lack of recognition

Seven of Wands Reversed

Being bullied

Without force

Backing off

Wanting to be stronger

Being on shaky ground

Weakness

Being unsure

Hesitation

Not knowing where you stand

Admitting defeat

Lack of trust

Avoiding a fight

Avoiding a challenge

Letting others get the better of you

Being defensive

Putting up with abuse

Eight of Wands Reversed

Going backwards

Turning back time

Missing your mark

Backfiring

Awaiting news

Hidden truth

Returns

More preparation required

Setbacks

The need for focus

Hiding away

Out bid

Backing out

Sending something back

The need to speed up

Aiming too high

Nine of Wands Reversed

Fatigued

Letting your guard down

Lowering walls

Lack of stamina

Not persisting

Giving up

Slowing down

Feeling caged

Being held up

Application denied

Defeat

Putting yourself first

Waiting for a break

Extended prison sentence

Need for caution

Ten of Wands Reversed

Shirking responsibility

Dropping your bundle

Taking the easy way out

Passing the buck

Doing the bare minimum

Delegating

Going with the flow

Finding a better way

Leaving a mess

Being unaccountable

A narrow escape

Pain free

Simplifying things

Managing to hold it together

Working smarter, not harder

Page of Wands Reversed

Creative block

Lethargy

Fearful

Laziness

Wasted talent

Avoiding a challenge

Lacking drive

Unambitious

Self-doubt

Doubtful

Follower

Unadventurous

Passive

Immaturity

Having difficulty expressing yourself

Needing motivation

Doesn't like to be Stretched

Knight of Wands Reversed

Lacks tact

Can be reckless

Troublemaker

Promiscuous

Puts others down

Looks for the easy way out

Bad tempered

Has a large ego

Cowardly

Argumentative

Tends to act without thinking

Lacks commitment

Insulting

Superficial

Delay in receiving information

Misdirected energy

Queen of Wands Reversed

Name dropper

Seeks attention

Vain

Lacks confidence

Ill natured

Sore loser

Wants to win

Can be lazy and unkept

May do things excessively

Manipulating

Hard to please

Easily angered

Likes to get his/her own way

Jealous

Likes to show off

Will use charm to manipulate

Will try to take credit for the actions of others

King of Wands Reversed

Bluffs his way through

Lacks creativity

Easily angered

Unoriginal

Self-absorbed

Unattractive

Selfish

Weak

Intimidating

Bully

Lacks conviction

Can't commit

Domineering

Unromantic

Manipulative

Worries what others think of him/her

Won't over-extend himself

Ace of Pentacles Reversed

Losing money

Missed opportunities

Insecurity

Delay in commencement

Unsupported

Feeling fragile

Fragile relationship

Misjudgement

Time to start exercising

Running on empty

Instability

Weakened Immune system

Irresponsible

Low bank balance

Time to invest some money or time

Unconventional plan

Two of Pentacles Reversed

Imbalanced

Not coping

Inflexible

Unresolved issues

Overindulging

Withdrawn

Obstacles

Resisting new ideas

At a low point

Not being available

Impatient

Problematic

Limitations

Coming across a lot of problems

Feeling that life is upside down

Three of Pentacles Reversed

Unco-operative

Lack of co-ordination

Slacking off

Bad workmanship

Lack of preparation

Lack of team- work

Delays in completion

Unmotivated

Deals fall over

Inexperience

Being divided

Setbacks

Counter-productive

Being out of your depth

No attention to detail

Four of Pentacles Reversed

Lack of control

Unable to save money

Missing out

Losing money

Disorganisation

Erratic behaviour

Spending up

Lacking structure

Weakness

Gambler

Spendthrift

Investment

Fraud

embezzlement

Not keeping up with health checks

Looking too far ahead

Unreliable

Concealed

Five of Pentacles Reversed

Sunshine after rain

Better times ahead

Taking better care of yourself

Regaining energy

Receiving charity

Government assistance

Windfall

Being welcomed back

Forgiveness

Having a good friend when needed

Light at the end of the tunnel

Getting approval

Silver lining

Slow recovery from being ill

Receiving a helping hand

Six of Pentacles Reversed

Stinginess

Lack of support

Losing control

Being disrespected

Having little influence

Being left to your own devices

Can't pay the rent

Left out of the will

Being turned away

Refused entry

No care factor

Not getting your wish

Unable to make ends meet

Holding on to what you've got

Seven of Pentacles Reversed

Minimum growth

Declining health

Staying put

Limitations

Mismanagement

Lack of diversity

Downturn

Missing out

Overworked

Unapproachable

Taking your eye off the prize

Underpaid

Neglect

Losing what you've worked hard for

Eight of Pentacles Reversed

Not producing results

Taking time off

Being unreliable

Bad craftmanship

Lack of commitment

Missing details

Uncommitted

Loose ends

Unmotivated

Laziness

Not having all the facts

Shirking responsibility

Leaving things out

Lack of research

Nine of Pentacles Reversed

Undisciplined

Not able to retire yet

Inability to cope

Needing assistance

Working beyond retirement

Unrefined

Needing to be around others

Discontented

Insecure

Going without luxuries

Lacking intact and manners

Insufficient funds

Over working

Ten of Pentacles Reversed

Financial insecurity

Disinherited

Redundancy

Business losses

Living for today

Non-conforming

Shunting tradition

Selling the family home

Unable to retire

Family breakdown

Experiencing bad luck

Poverty

Dysfunctional family

Page of Pentacles Reversed

Untrustworthy

Lacking intensity

Rejection

Not sticking to your plans

Unachievable goals

Undependable

Spreading rumours

Letting others down

Bad news

Ungrounded

Suspended dreams

Immaturity

Without credibility

Unconventional

Knight of Pentacles Reversed

Being stuck in a rut

Stubborn

Avoiding hard work

Obsessed

Held back by fear

Dislike change

Uninspiring individual

Missed opportunities

Playing it safe

Laziness and procrastination

The need to step out of your comfort zone

Boredom

Queen of Pentacles Reversed

Unsupportive

Unwelcoming

Smothering

Over-spending

Unavailable

Misplaced generosity

Can be disloyal

Impatient

Disregard for health or exercise

Anti-social

Secretive

Frugal

Prefers to receive than to give

King of Pentacles Reversed

Lacks management skills

Under achiever

Tyrannical

Gambling addiction

Moody

Lacks competence

Unreliable

Non charitable

Unstable

Corrupt

Can be unstable and unpredictable

Has an unhealthy attachment to money

Ace of Cups Reversed

Inability to express feelings

Unsympathetic

Lacking intimacy

Feeling alone

Unable to be affectionate

Feeling drained

No emotional connection

Unattached

Not caring anymore

Running out of patience

Lacking spirituality

Not trusting your intuition

Feeling emotional

Two of Cups Reversed

Relationship break up

Lack of attraction

Feeling neglected

Disharmony

Disagreements

Letting go

Holding a grudge

Going backwards

Deal falls through

Bad date

Inability to reach an agreement

Bad choices

Moving on

Inability to work together

Three of Cups Reversed

Lacking energy

Being excluded

Over-indulging

Missing friends

Party crashers

Taking life too seriously

The need to socialise

Letting the team down

Feeling miserable

Cancellation

Feeling isolated

Over working

Withdrawing from society

Four of Cups Reversed

Putting others before yourself

The need for meditation

Procrastination

Refusing help

The need to make an effort

The need for attention

Confusion

Seeking therapy

Emotional pain

Looking for a project

Time to make choice

Taking the easy option

Taking a broader view

Five of Cups Reversed

Letting go of pain

Slow recovery

Unresolved issues

Renewed hope

Working through problems

Being grateful for what you have

Going to therapy

Opening up

Releasing pain

Seeing the light

Building self-esteem

Putting the past behind you

Coming through a particularly difficult period

Six of Cups Revered

Troubled childhood

Acting unkindly

Being greedy

Feeling trapped

Neglect

Having bad intentions

Being a bad influence

Not having fun

Detention

Childless

Bullying

Feeling guilty

Taking more than you're entitled to

Mixing with the wrong crowd

Seven of Cups Reversed

Running out options

Feeling empowered

Revelation

Feeling enlightened

Getting over an addiction

Breaking a fever

Investigating health treatments

Feeling at a low point

Hallucinations or drug use

Compulsive lying

Giving up on dreams

Being distracted

Knowing exactly what you want

Recognising a good thing when you see it

Eight of Cups Reversed

Staying in a bad situation

Feeling like there is no way out

Fear of change

Boredom

Being needy or clingy

Low self-esteem

Unfinished business

Tying up loose ends

Second chances

One last attempt

Trying to make it work

Not giving up

Wanting commitment

Returning to a place that holds memories

Nine of Cups Reversed

Feeling unsatisfied

Not getting your wish

Bad catering

No one to celebrate with

Giving up alcohol

Feeling down

Shattered dreams

Restlessness

Intoxication

Therapy session

Not getting your way

Runner up

Something standing in the way of happiness

All dressed up with no place to go

Ten of Cups Reversed

Experiencing sadness

Conflict

Unhappy at home

Arguments

Insecurity

Divorce

Mixed marriage

Abuse

Misfortune

Marriage counselling

Miscarriage

Ingratitude

Inability to conceive a child

Lack of support

Mishap that affects the family

Unable to get the family together

Page of Cups Reversed

Sad news

Unemotional

Jealousy

Writers block

Immaturity

Deception

Insincere friend

Bullying behaviour

Attention seeker

Unsympathetic

Lacking intimacy

Judgemental

Pessimism

Easily influenced by social media

Uncommunicative

Lacking intuition

Knight of Cups Reversed

Jealousy

Melodramatic

Moody

Overactive imagination

Temperamental

Mental illness

Overly sensitive

Confused sexual orientation

Overly anxious

Easily offended

Revoked invitation

Tends to embellish the truth

Tends to exaggerate

Disappointing news

Queen of Cups Reversed

Places conditions on relationships

Lacks respect

Spiritual blockages

Unkind

Lacks intuition

Lacks compassion

Unempathetic

Can be blunt

Need for honesty

The need to develop your senses

Selfishness

Lacks closeness

Impatient

Can tend toward being manipulative

King of Cups Reversed

Lacking wisdom

Misunderstands people

Confuses issues

Easily angered

Lacks composure

Acting nervously

Easily upset

Uncharitable

Emotional blockages

Narrow-minded

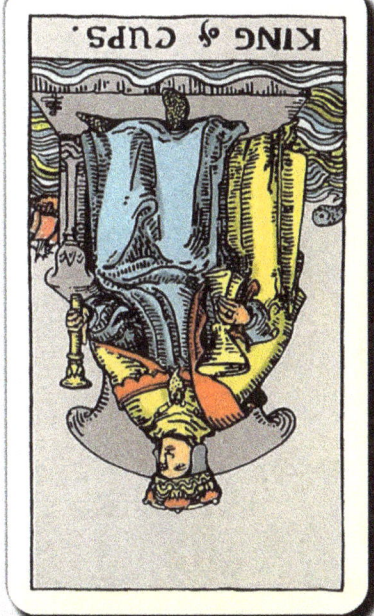

Intolerant

Insincere

Uncomfortable in social settings

Ace of Swords Reversed

Losing

Being subjective

Injustice

Being deceived

Confusion

Misunderstanding

Dishonesty

Unreal

Irresponsible

Lacking intelligence

Illogical

Uninspired

Unfocused

Miscommunication

Doing the wrong thing

Two of Swords Reversed

Listening   Embracing problems

Moving forward   Causing a stir

Willing to act   Decision making

Recognising the warning signs

Having an opinion

Facing facts   Being open to all possibilities

Admitting fears

Showing emotion

Being in touch with your feelings

Three of Swords Reversed

Healing

Good news after bad

Reconciliation

Treating depression

Being given support

The worst is over

Holding on to grief

Moving on from a relationship breakdown

Stirring up painful memories

Watching a sad movie

Recovering a sentimental item

Therapy

Recovery from heart surgery

Getting over a disappointment

Sunshine after rain

Four of Swords Reversed

Exhaustion

Lack of appreciation

Confusion

Not taking time to recover

Not being recognised for your efforts

Not getting enough rest

The need to finalise things

Being over stimulated

Not trusting your intuition

Over thinking

The need to assess a situation

The need for meditation   Instability

Five of Swords Reversed

The need for self-care

Resolution

Having integrity

Mending bridges

Knowing right from wrong

Standing up to bullying

Compromise

Doing what's ethical

Being caught out

Wanting revenge

Avoiding an argument

Putting others first

Compromise

Walking away from a fight

Six of Swords Reversed

Blockages around healing

Disrupted travel

Bumpy ride

Unable to move on

Having nowhere to go

Restrictions

Troubles in water

Turbulence

Setbacks with mental health

Feelings of hopelessness

Not coping

Bad weather

Sinking

Delays in escaping troubled times

Seven of Swords Reversed

Uncovering a crime

Exposing deception

Spreading rumours

Sneaky behaviour

Getting caught out

Controlling behaviour

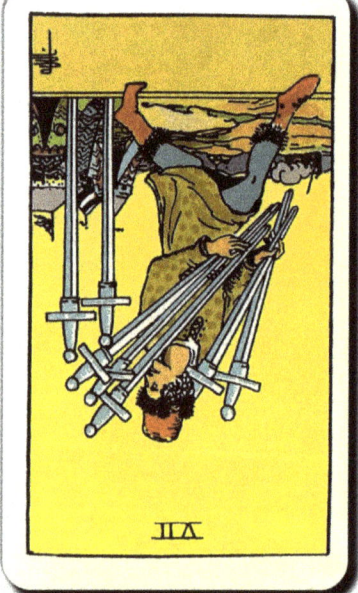

Going undercover

Being held accountable

Stealing

Going behind someone's back

Watch your back

Feelings of suspicion

Distorting the truth

Covert dealings

Eight of Swords Reversed

Finding answers

Escape from reality

Overcoming fear

Taking the pressure off

Removing restrictions

Beating depression

Taking back the power

Surviving

Release from prison

Walking away

Clearing the mind

Taking action

Looking for a way out

Taking responsibility for yourself

Nine of Swords Reversed

Overcoming insomnia

Managing fears

Recovery

Moving on from troubled times

Accepting help

Letting worries take you over

Managing pain

Overcoming stress

Breakdown

Sacrificing sleep

Being too hard on yourself

Managing depression and anxiety

Finding joy again

Ten of Swords Reversed

Not letting anyone get to you

Watch your back

Fighting back

The need to put yourself first

Not giving up

Being up against it

Proving you were right

The need for bravery

Proving your worth

Being defensive

Exaggeration

Inner strength

Remaining in a negative mind-set

Page of Swords Reversed

Gossiping

Dishonesty

Deceit

Lack of research

Favouritism

Creating confusion

Wrong-doing

Illogical

Feeling low

Feeling uninspired

Being tricked

Missing out on a scholarship

Playing mind games

Being uncommunicative

Blockages with learning and study

Knight of Swords Reversed

Being tactless and rude

Bad manners

Disruptive news

Indiscretion

Domineering

Sarcasm

Unfeeling

Criticism

Restraint

Accidents

Feeling down

Cutting words

Out of control

Impetuous

Not acting quickly enough

Inappropriate behaviour

Queen of Swords Reversed

Tends to exaggerate

Unrealistic

Lacking a sense of humour

Secretive

Narrowminded

Self-righteous

Breaking rules

Inability to think clearly

Lacking experience

Dishonesty

Vindictive

Judgemental

Talks about people behind their back

Wants things their own way

King of Swords Reversed

Lacking knowledge

Clouded judgement

Uninspiring

Creative block

Acting unethically

Shady deal

Uncommunicative

Can be scathing

Wants things their own way

Boring personality type

Unapproachable

Writer's block

Inability to analyse a situation

Conclusion

'And one day, just like that….
You'll re-discover your inner warrior.
You'll snatch your power back.
And the whole game will change.'

If you have bought and read this book, I am hoping that it has been, and will continue to be, helpful to you in your tarot learning journey. I have written it based on what I would have loved having access to when I was learning because, at the time, it seemed such an insurmountable task.

I have tried to limit the amount of text within this book knowing that pages and pages of words, when you are starting out, can make the process daunting and also be difficult to retain. If at first, you only use the key meaning references along with some of the exercises, numerology and colour, you will then be more well equipped to absorb further information, use your intuition to discover deeper messages, and set out on your own quest for the many vast and varied elements of the tarot that may interest you. Tarot can be used in so many facets of our lives from finding missing objects to communicating with loved ones who have passed on, and much more.

The vast majority of us who are passionate about tarot and devote an enormous amount of time and energy mastering the practice, do so out of a desire to help others.

There is so much satisfaction in knowing that the person you have guided through difficult times, given hope to, or even just listened to, lets you know how pivotal the advice of the cards was to them and to their sense of security.

My own journey of having tarot cards read for me started nearly thirty years ago when I discovered a remarkable tarot reader who managed to give me genuine and constructive advice for all that was happening in my life at the time. I would travel a great distance to see her yearly, and sometimes every six months or so. Eventually over the years as times changed, she would travel to see me, doing readings in my own home. Her husband would drive her, and it wasn't long before relationships with my whole family were formed. She has recently retired, and her wonderful husband has passed away and will be missed by us all. She has been a brilliant mentor for me and her encouragement of my tarot reading journey has inspired and motivated me to overcome many fears and self-doubt.

Tarot can bring so many wonderful and interesting people into your life and broaden your knowledge on innumerable topics and subjects. This in turn, can offer you the expertise and the means to give guidance to others.

It is also a great guiding tool for your own life, often confirming what your intuition tells you.

I encourage you, as I've said earlier, to join any social media groups as they can offer an invaluable source of free knowledge extended by many experienced tarot experts, and also provide you with support should you have any questions of your own. I've also known people to have gained some long-lasting friendships as an additional bonus to their tarot learning experience.

My last words of advice are to follow your heart if tarot is something you are passionate about, as I was. Don't be disillusioned if you are not supported by friends or family members in your decision to study tarot. My immediate family and some friends were extremely supportive of me, but there are always those few who will disappoint you with their lack of understanding or uneasiness with tarot in general. If you are determined and committed to learning, you will remain focused and enthusiastic and become the incredible tarot reader you were always meant to be. It won't happen overnight, but it will happen.

> **'Believe in yourself. You are braver than you think,**
> **More gifted than you know,**
> **And capable of more than you imagine'**

www.ingramcontent.com/pod-product-compliance
Lightning Source LLC
Chambersburg PA
CBHW051535010526
44107CB00064B/2732